FREE STYLE 2020

Discover Enhanced Nutritional Cooking With Proven Acid Reflux and Gastric Sleeve Free Style Cookbook For Healing After Surgery - With Karen Nosrat Emily Vuong Simon Walker

Simon Davis
Jelly C. Powell
Heidi Naquin

Table of Contents

PART 1 3
- CHAPTER 1: WHAT IS THE FREESTYLE WAY? 4
- CHAPTER 2: BREAKFAST FAVOURITES 7
- CHAPTER 3: LUNCH FAVORITES 20
- CHAPTER 4: SCRUMPTIOUS DINNER CHOICES: BEEF – FISH & SEAFOOD 34
- CHAPTER 5: SCRUMPTIOUS DINNER CHOICES: PORK & POULTRY 42
- CHAPTER 6: DELICIOUS SIDES 51
- CHAPTER 7: 21-DAY MEAL PLAN 60
- CONCLUSION 66
- INDEX FOR THE RECIPES 67

PART 2 70
- INTRODUCTION 71
- CHAPTER 1: CHRONIC ACID REFLUX & ITS SERIOUS HEALTH IMPLICATIONS 72
- CHAPTER 2: THE ROLE OF FIBRE, PREBIOTICS AND PROBIOTICS 79
- CHAPTER 3: UNDERSTANDING THE ROLE OF PROTEINS, CARBS, AND FATS IN HEALING ACID DAMAGE 86
- CHAPTER 4: EXERCISE TO REDUCE ACID REFLUX 91
- CHAPTER 5: HOW TO LIVE A REFLUX FREE LIFE? 93

PART 3 98
- CHAPTER 1: IS WEIGHT LOSS SURGERY RIGHT FOR YOU? 99
- CHAPTER 2: TYPES OF GASTRIC SLEEVE SURGERIES 103
- CHAPTER 3: THE RECOVERY PHASE 107
- CHAPTER 4: RECIPES FOR RECOVERY 111

CONCLUSION 135

PART 1

Chapter 1: What is The Freestyle Way?

As you begin your journey using the Freestyle techniques, you will learn it utilizes the elements of calories in and calories out. The point system assigns specific points based on the nutritional and calorie content. Your activity level also influences how the points are assigned to offset against the food points.

One excellent online resource to discover your points is available at "healthyweightforum.org/eng/calculators/ww-points-allowed/" The information involved includes your gender, age, activity level, weight, height, and how many pounds you want to lose. The math is calculated for you to show how many points you can consume on your meal plan daily.

For example, a 65-year old woman who has a sedentary lifestyle, is 5'1" tall, 174 lbs. who wants to lose 10 pounds is allowed 24 points for the first 2 weeks and 23 points for the next 3 weeks.

All you need to do is add the points for additional optional or toppings that are not included in the recipe. Each food added to the product will possibly raise the content of fat or sugar. Proteins are calculated into the equation to help lower the points.

The goal is to get you on the right track of choosing leaner proteins and eating more fruits and vegetables with each meal. By increasing these food items, you are lowering the unhealthy fats and consuming less sugar. You will be surprised by many of the foods that contain -0- points. It's hard to believe they are diet-friendly foods!

Use your enclosed 21-day plan as a guideline to get your body in tune with the new way of eating healthier. It won't take long before you are inspired. Your family and friends will surely enjoy the tastier techniques used for food preparation. You will also love all of the new zero foods!

Zero Point Fruits

Enjoy most fruits in moderation - only because the calories can add up quickly. The only exceptions to the rule are plantains and avocados. Consider this as you prepare your smoothie, if you add any additional fruits - be sure to consider any possible points involved. This includes frozen or fresh fruit, as well as jarred or canned. Just remember to choose the ones packaged without added sugar.

Zero Point Vegetables

Many veggies are -0- points on the new Freestyle plan. However, as you prepare your meal, be sure to take into accounts the oil and butter used as you make the vegetables. Enjoy canned, fresh or frozen mushy peas, potatoes, parsnips, cassava, yuca, yams, sweet potatoes, and olives - without additional fats, oil, or sugars.

Zero Point Spices & Other Condiments

You can choose from many items including low-sugar condiments and spices. For example, enjoy items such as fresh or rubs, vinegar, broth, dried spices, hot sauce, mustard, salsa, and capers.

Remember, the points consumed will also depend on the amount you are using in your recipe. They may be zero points for a small serving, but collectively, as they are used in the recipe, they may contain more points.

Other Foods To Enjoy Freestyle

- Boneless & skinless chicken breast and turkey
- Ground lean chicken and turkey
- Thinly sliced deli chicken or turkey breast
- All shellfish and fish (excluding smoked or dried fish)
- Canned fish packed in brine or water
- Regular and smoked tofu
- Eggs
- Plain soy yogurt
- Plain Greek yogurt
- Fresh – frozen - canned beans and lentils that are packed without oil or sugar (Ex. Lentils, pinto beans, split peas, chickpeas, black beans, kidney beans, soybeans, and more)

Chapter 2: Breakfast Favourites

No matter what you are craving, just remember, breakfast is considered the most important meal of the day. So, enjoy each one of these selections as you adjust to your new way of meal preparation!

Baked Omelet

Freestyle Points: 2

Yields: 4 Servings

Ingredients:

- Egg whites – 3
- Large eggs - 3
- Greek yogurt - plain fat-free – 2 tbsp.
- Pepper - .25 tsp.
- Salt - .125 tsp.
- Onion - .25 cup
- Bell peppers - .25 cup
- Grated parmesan cheese - .25 cup
- Cubed ham - .5 cup
- Broccoli florets – 1 cup
- Baby spinach leaves – 2 cups
- For the Garnish: Green onion – 1
- Also Needed: -10-inch skillet

Preparation Method:

1. Warm up the temperature setting in the oven to 400°F.
2. Chop the veggies. Whip the yogurt, eggs, pepper, and salt until frothy using a hand mixer.
3. Warm up the skillet using the med-high setting and spray with oil to prevent sticking. Add the broccoli, peppers, ham, and onions. Lower the temperature to the medium heat setting. Continue cooking for approximately five minutes.
4. Toss in the spinach and continue cooking until wilted. Blend in the green onions and add the mixed eggs. Sprinkle with the parmesan.
5. Cook 10 minutes on the stovetop. Move it to the oven for 10 to 15 additional minutes until the eggs are done and set.
6. Garnish with a few green onions and parmesan cheese before serving.

Banana Roll-Ups

Freestyle Points:2

Yields: 1 Serving

Ingredients:

- Whole wheat bread – low-cal – 1 slice
- Medium peeled banana - .5 of 1
- Salt-free chunky peanut butter - 1.5 tsp.

Preparation Method:

1. Use a rolling pin or wine bottle as a substitute to flatten the bread.
2. Apply the peanut butter to one side of the bread. Add the banana.
3. Roll it up and slice into 3-4 segments.
4. Enjoy any time.

Broccoli Cheddar Egg Muffins

Freestyle Points: 2

Yields: 6 Servings

Ingredients:

- Egg whites - 4
- Whole eggs- 8
- Dijon mustard -.5 tbsp. - optional
- Broccoli – 2 cups **
- Shredded cheddar cheese - .75 cups
- Pepper and salt – to your liking
- Diced green onions - 2

** Use either fresh and steamed or defrosted and frozen broccoli.

Preparation Method:

1. Warm up the oven to 350°F. Prepare 6 muffin tins with paper liners or cooking spray.
2. Whisk all of the eggs, salt, pepper, and mustard. Blend in the green onions, broccoli, and cheese.
3. Divide up the batter and bake for 12-14 minutes.
4. Serve when they are puffy and thoroughly cooked.

Cinnamon-Apple French Toast

Freestyle Points: 4

Yields: 4 Servings

Ingredients:

- Liquid egg whites – 1.33 cups
- 1% milk – 1 cup
- Eggs – 4
- Cinnamon – 2 tsp.
- Apples – 2
- Slices of low-calorie bread – 8
- Also Needed: 9 x 13 casserole dish

Preparation Method:

1. Peel and dice the apples. Grease the baking dish with cooking spray. Prepare the oven temperature to 350°F.
2. Using a microwavable dish to combine and cook the cinnamon and apples for three minutes.
3. Line the baking dish with bread slices and a layer of cooked apples.
4. Whisk the egg whites and milk. Pour over the bread. Bake 45 minutes. Serve and enjoy with your favorite toppings.

Country Cottage Pancakes

Freestyle Points: 3

Yields: 4 Servings

Ingredients:

- Low-fat cottage cheese – 1 cup
- Medium eggs – 8
- Coconut flour – 4 tbsp.
- Bicarb of soda - .5 tsp.
- Almond flour – 4 tbsp.
- Grated zest of lemon – 1 tsp.
- Kosher salt – A pinch
- Vanilla essence - .5 tsp.
- Sweetened almond milk – 4 tbsp.

Preparation Method:

1. In a blender; combine all of the fixings – excluding the almond milk for now. Blitz until smooth.
2. Lightly spritz a skillet with cooking oil spray. Warm it up using medium-high temperature setting.
3. Prepare in four batches – one at a time. Flip only once, when the pancakes start bubbling. Continue cooking and serve immediately.

Egg & Sausage Muffins

Freestyle Points: 1

Yields: 20 Servings

Ingredients:

- Lean turkey breakfast sausage – 1 lb.
- Liquid egg whites – 3 cups
- Minced cloves of garlic - 2
- Green chilis – 4 oz. – 1 can - mild or hot
- Small chopped onion - 1
- Hash browns – 3 cups
- Black pepper – to your liking
- Sea salt – 1.5 tsp.

Preparation Method:

1. Warm up the oven to 375°F. Prepare 20 muffin tins with some cooking spray.
2. Cook the sausage on the stovetop using the med-high heat setting. As it breaks apart, stir in the onions, garlic, and chilies. Remove when the onions have softened.
3. Prepare the same skillet with a spritz of cooking spray. Toss in the hash browns, salt, and pepper the way you like it. Simmer 3-4 minutes. Fold in the eggs and combine well.
4. Dump the prepared batter into the tins. Bake 15-18 minutes. Check the centers for doneness using the toothpick test.

Egg & Veggie Scramble

Freestyle Points: 1

Yields: 6 Servings

Ingredients:

- Extra-virgin olive oil – 1.5 tbsp.
- Diced tomato - 1
- Large eggs - 6
- Baby spinach – 3 cups
- Minced garlic clove - 1
- Red or purple diced onion - .5 of 1
- Black pepper and Kosher salt – 1 tsp. of each
- 2% sharp cheddar cheese - .5 cup

Preparation Method:

1. Whisk the eggs, pepper, and salt.
2. Warm up the olive oil in a skillet. Toss in the spinach, tomato, onions, and garlic. Simmer until done or about 5-7 minutes.
3. Pour in the eggs and simmer 3-4 minutes – stirring occasionally. When set, remove from the burner and add the cheese on top. Serve and enjoy.

Hard-Boiled Eggs in the Instant Pot

Freestyle Points: -0-

Yields: Varies

Ingredients:

- Water – 1 cup
- Eggs - your choice in a single layer

Preparation Method:

1. Measure out the water and add to the pot. Gently add the eggs to the rack basket. Close the lid and set the timer for 3-5 minutes (high-pressure).
2. Natural release the pressure for 5 minutes and quick release the remainder of the built-up steam pressure.
3. Arrange the eggs in a cold-water dish to cool. A few ice cubes will speed the process. Wait 5-10 minutes before peeling.

Muffin Tin Eggs

Freestyle Points: 1

Yields: 6 Servings

Ingredients

- Eggs – 1 dozen
- Fat-free ground turkey breast - .5 lb.
- Diced green bell pepper – 1
- Steak seasoning – ex. Montreal Blend – 1 tsp.
- Red pepper flakes - .25 tsp.
- Black pepper and salt - .5 tsp. each
- Sage - .5 tsp.
- Marjoram - .25 tsp.
- Also Needed: -12-cup muffin tin

Preparation Method:

1. Set the oven temperature to 350°F. Prepare the muffin tin with cooking spray.
2. Spray the skillet and add the turkey, pepper flakes, black pepper, marjoram, salt, and sage. Cook for 7-10 minutes. Stir often to prevent sticking.
3. In a large mixing container, combine the steak seasoning and eggs - mixing well (2-3 min.) until fluffy. Blend in the diced pepper.
4. Once the turkey mixture is done, spoon into the tins and add the egg mixture. Fill about 3/4 full and bake for 30 minutes in the hot oven.

Tropical Breakfast Pie

Freestyle Points: 5

Yields: 4 Servings

Ingredients:

- Refrigerated biscuit dough – 7.5 oz.
- Unsweetened shredded coconut – 2 tbsp.
- Granulated sugar - .5 tsp.
- Fresh pineapple – 1 cup
- Also Needed: 8-inch-square casserole dish

Preparation Method:

1. Warm up the oven in advance to 350°F.
2. Lightly coat the casserole dish with a splash of cooking spray. Break apart the dough into 10 portions and slice into quarters.
3. Load a Ziploc-type bag with the sugar and coconut. Shake well and add the dough bits. Shake gently, but well to coat.
4. Place the biscuits into the dish and garnish with the diced pineapple.
1. Place in the preheated oven. Bake for 25 minutes.

Zucchini Noodles & Poached Eggs – Instant Pot

Freestyle Points: 4

Yields: 3 Servings

Ingredients for the Noodles:

- Olive oil – 1 tsp.
- Large spiralized zucchinis – 2
- Chopped cauliflower – 1 cup
- Garlic cloves – 2
- Small chopped onion – 1
- Large eggs – 2

Ingredients for the Seasoning:

- Ground smoked paprika - .5 tsp.
- Salt – 1 tsp.
- Black pepper - .5 tsp.
- Finely chopped chives – 1 tsp.
- Also Needed: Spiralizer

Preparation Method:

1. Rinse the zucchinis and discard the tips. Spiralize and set aside.
2. Plug in the Instant Pot. Give it a spritz of the olive oil in the stainless-steel insert. Add in the noodles and water and cook for 5 minutes. Set aside and cover.

3. Stir in the chopped cauliflower with a sprinkle of salt. Pour enough water to cover, and secure the top. Set the timer for 5 minutes using the high-pressure setting.
4. Quick release the pressure and add to the food processor with the salt, pepper, paprika, onion, and garlic. Blend until smooth.
5. Return the rest of the fixings into the Instant Pot and stir. Add the eggs on top and saute for around 3 minutes or until the eggs are cooked to your preference. Serve with a sprinkle of chives.

Chapter 3: lunch favorites

Whether you want some quick chicken, a bowl of soup or a salad; you'll find it here!

Chicken

Asian Turkey Stir-Fry

Freestyle Points: 2

Yields: 4 Servings

Ingredients:

- Asian vegetable mix - 16 oz. bag
- Ground turkey - 99% lean - 1 lb.
- Soy sauce – 4 tbsp.
- Minced cloves of garlic – 2
- Minced ginger – 2 tbsp.
- Coconut oil – 1 tbsp.
- Rice vinegar – 2 tbsp.
- Sesame oil – 1 tbsp.

Preparation Method:

1. Warm up the oil using med-high heat. Next, add the turkey, garlic, and ginger.
2. After the turkey is fully cooked; just dump the veggies into the pan. Next, cook it for 4 to 5 minutes or until tender.
3. Pour in the soy sauce and vinegar. Cook for two more minutes. Taste and add seasoning or soy sauce as desired before serving.

Buffalo Chicken Tenders

Freestyle Points: 5

Yields: 6 Servings

Ingredients:

- Chicken breasts – 1 lb.
- Panko breadcrumbs – 1 cup
- Flour - .25 cup
- Eggs – 3
- Red hot sauce - .33 cup
- Brown sugar - .5 cup
- Garlic powder - .5 tsp.
- Water – 3 tbsp.

Preparation Method:

1. Set the oven setting to 425°F.
2. Slice the chicken into strips and pound to 1/2-inch thickness for even cooking and tenderness. Toss into a zipper-type baggie along with the flour. Shake well.
3. Add the breadcrumbs in one dish and the eggs in another.
4. Dredge the chicken in the eggs, then the breadcrumbs. Arrange on a baking sheet and spray with a misting of cooking oil. Bake 20 minutes.
5. Prepare the sauce with the rest of the fixings in a small saucepan.
6. Enjoy the tenders with the sauce and your favorite side of veggies.

Salads

Caesar Salad – Instant Pot

Freestyle Points: 5

Yields: 5 Servings

Ingredients:

- Chicken breasts – 1 lb.
- Iceberg lettuce – 1 cup
- Pepper & Salt – to taste

Ingredients for the Dressing:

- Crushed garlic cloves - 2
- Greek yogurt - .25 cup
- Low-fat mayonnaise – 2 tsp.
- White wine vinegar – 1 tbsp.
- Freshly grated Italian Grana Padano cheese – 2 oz.

Preparation Method:

1. Combine the dressing fixings and set to the side.
2. Prepare the Instant Pot insert and spritz with some cooking oil. Warm it up using the saute function. Add the chicken with the pepper and salt. Saute three to four minutes per side. Take it out of the pot and set those aside also.
3. Roughly chop the lettuce and toss in the chicken with a sprinkle of the dressing.
4. Serve immediately and enjoy.

Ham Salad

Freestyle Points: 2

Yields: 4 Servings

Ingredients:

- Cooked – chopped ham – 1 cup
- Mango chutney – 1 tbsp.
- Onion powder – 2 tsp.
- Light mayonnaise – 2 tbsp.
- Dried mustard – 2 tsp.
- Non-fat plain Greek yogurt – 2 tbsp.

Preparation Method:

1. Pulse the fixings (omit the ham or not) in a processor until smooth.
2. Place the container in the refrigerator for about 30 minutes.
3. Add a dish of cucumber slices for a -0- points.

Pear & Blue Cheese Salad

Freestyle Points: 3

Servings: 4

Ingredients:

- White wine vinegar – 2 tbsp.
- Pear nectar - .25 cup
- Walnut oil – 2 tbsp.
- Ground black pepper - .125 tsp.
- Ground ginger - .125 tsp.
- Medium green pears – sliced - 3
- Torn mesclun greens – 10 cups
- Dijon mustard – 1 tsp.
- Honey – 1 tsp.
- Broken walnuts - .5 cup
- Crumbled blue cheese - .5 cup

Preparation Method:

1. Whisk the walnut oil, nectar, vinegar, honey, pepper, ginger, and mustard until well mixed. Set to the side for now.
2. Combine the rest of the ingredients and add the dressing. Toss well to coat. Chill in the fridge before time to eat.

Tuna Salad with Cranberries – Onion & Celery

Freestyle Points: 3

Yields: 5 Servings

Ingredients for the Seasoning – to taste:

- Red pepper flakes
- Freshly cracked black pepper
- Sea salt

Ingredients for the Tuna Salad:

- White tuna in spring water – 16 oz. can
- Low-fat mayonnaise – 3 tbsp.
- Light sour cream – 3 tbsp.
- Celery - .5 cup
- Red onion - .25 cup
- Dried cranberries - .25 cup
- Lemon juice – 1 tbsp.
- Cored apple - 1

Preparation Method:

1. Drain the tuna, mince the onion, and chop the celery. Core and thinly slice the apples.
2. Squeeze a fresh lemon for fresh juice. Combine the seasonings. Also, combine the salad fixings.
3. When ready to serve, garnish as desired and enjoy.

Soups

Beef Chili – Slow-Cooker

Freestyle Points: 4

Yields: 12 Servings

Ingredients:

- Lean ground beef – 1 lb.
- Diced bell peppers - 2
- Minced cloves of garlic
- Cumin – 2 tsp.
- Diced tomatoes – 1 can – 28 oz.
- Green chilis – canned .25 cup
- Kidney beans – 15 oz.
- Onion – 1 chopped
- Chili powder – 2 tbsp.
- Tomato paste – 2 tbsp.
- Salt – to taste

Preparation Method:

1. Warm up a skillet using the med-high temperature setting. Stir in the garlic and beef until browned (10 min. or so). Stir in the peppers and continue cooking 5 more minutes. Sprinkle with the cumin and chili powder.
2. Scoop the meat into the slow cooker with the remainder of the fixings. Stir and close the top. Prepare for eight to ten hours using the low-temperature setting.
3. When done, just taste test and adjust the seasonings to your liking.

Butternut Squash Soup

Freestyle Points: 1

Yields: 8 Servings

Ingredients:

- Raw cubed squash – 12 oz.
- Fat-free vegetable stock – 4 cups
- Green apple - .5 of 1
- Onion - .5 of 1
- Ground ginger – 1 pinch
- Black pepper & Salt – to taste
- Ground nutmeg – 1 pinch

Preparation Method:

1. Warm up a large stockpot and add the apple, onion, squash, and stock. Stir and cover until it boils. Then, reduce the temperature and remove the lid.
2. Continue cooking slowly for 10 minutes and puree with a blender. Give it a shake of salt, pepper, nutmeg, and ginger.
3. Serve and enjoy.

Chicken-Parmesan Soup

Freestyle Points: 3

Yields: 8 Servings

Ingredients:

- Olive oil – 1 tbsp.
- Minced cloves of garlic - 3
- Diced onion - 1
- Crushed tomatoes – 15 oz.
- Chicken stock – 6 cups
- Chicken breasts- no bones or skin – 12 oz.
- Part-skim mozzarella cheese – 1.5 cups
- Grated parmesan – 2 tbsp.
- Salt – 1 tsp.
- Red pepper flakes - .5 tsp.
- Dried parsley – 1 tsp.
- Black pepper - .5 tsp.

Preparation Method:

1. Prepare the stockpot using the med-high setting and add the oil. When warm, toss in the onions. Simmer 6 minutes. Toss in the garlic and continue cooking one additional minute.
2. Stir in the stock and tomatoes. Once it boils; just lower the heat setting. Remove the skin and bones from the chicken and add to the pot with the rest of the ingredients.
3. Simmer until the cheese is melted and serve.

Fish & Shrimp Stew

Freestyle Points: 2

Yields: 6 Servings

Ingredients:

- Minced garlic cloves - 2
- Crushed tomatoes – 28 oz. can
- Diced onion - 1
- Olive oil – 1 tbsp.
- Tomato paste – 3 tbsp.
- Parsley - .66 cup
- Fish stock – 14 oz.
- Clam juice – 8 oz.
- Ghee or butter – 2 tbsp.
- Basil – 5 tsp.
- Oregano - .5 tsp.
- Red pepper flakes - .25 tsp.
- Pepper and salt – to taste
- Raw shrimp – 1 lb.
- Cod – 2-inch pieces – 1.5 lb.

Preparation Method:

1. Use the medium heat setting to heat up the oil in a skillet. Toss in the onion and cook for five to seven minutes. Stir in the pepper flakes and garlic. Cook for another one to two minutes. Pour in the tomato paste and simmer one additional minute.

2. Stir in the tomatoes, clam juice, and fish stock. Simmer and add the basil, oregano, and butter. Simmer for 10-15 minutes.
3. Taste test and add the cod. Simmer for another 5 minutes and fold in the shrimp.
4. Continue cooking for 4-5 minutes until the shrimp is opaque.
5. Serve and enjoy.

Lentil Soup – Instant Pot

Freestyle Points: 1

Yield: 6 servings

Ingredients:

- Yellow onion - 1
- Carrots - 2
- Celery stalks - 2
- Diced tomatoes with juice – 1 can 15 oz.
- Garlic cloves - 2
- Curry powder – 1 tsp.
- Optional: Cayenne pepper - 1 pinch
- Ground cumin – 1 tsp.
- Dry green or brown lentils – 1 cup
- Water – 3 cups
- Freshly cracked black pepper – to taste
- Salt – 1 tsp. or more
- Fresh spinach - roughly chopped – 1 cup
- For Serving: Lemon slices

Preparation Method:

1. Plug in the Instant Pot to warm up for 10-15 minutes.
2. Peel and chop the onions, celery, and carrots. Mince the cloves of garlic and roughly chop the spinach.

3. Combine in the Instant Pot; the water, lentils, cayenne, curry, cumin, garlic, tomatoes, celery, onions, carrots, and a dash of black pepper. Stir well. (Omit the salt)
4. Close the top and lock it down. Set the timer for 10 minutes using the high-pressure setting. When it's done; just natural release the pressure for about 10 minutes and open the lid.
5. Stir and make sure the soup is well done. Add 1 teaspoon of salt with the spinach.
6. Serve warm after the spinach wilts. Garnish with a lemon wedge. Serve any time for up to a week when stored in the fridge in an airtight container.

Vegetable Soup

Freestyle Points: -0-

Yields: 6 Servings

Ingredients:

- Minced cloves of garlic - 3
- Chopped onion - 1
- Chicken stock - fat-free – 3 cups
- Frozen spinach – 10 oz.
- Diced zucchini - .5 cup
- Green beans - .5 cup
- Chopped carrots - .5 cup
- Tomato paste – 1 tbsp.
- Salt & Black pepper – to your liking
- Italian seasoning – 1 tsp.

Preparation Method:

1. Lightly spray a saucepan with some cooking oil spray. Warm it up using the medium heat setting and toss in the onion and garlic.
2. Cook about five minutes and stir in the tomato paste, stock, carrots, and green beans. Prepare for about 6 minutes.
3. Fold in the zucchini and simmer 5 additional minutes before adding the spinach to cook until heated.
4. Season to your liking and serve.

Chapter 4: scrumptious dinner choices: Beef – Fish & Seafood

Dinnertime is a special time of the day where your family can sit down and enjoy the conversations of daily events. From beef to fish and seafood, you will find a tempting dish to fit any occasion.

Beef Choices

Beef & Broccoli Stir-Fry

Freestyle Points: 3

Yields: 4 Servings

Ingredients:

- Lean sirloin beef - .75 lb.
- Table salt - .25 tsp.
- Cornstarch – divided – 2.5 tbsp.
- Canola oil – 2 tsp.
- Broccoli florets - 12 oz. bag – 5 cups
- Chicken broth – reduced-sodium – divided – 1cup
- Minced garlic – 2 tbsp.
- Soy sauce - .25 cup
- Water - .25 cup
- Red pepper flakes - .25 tsp.
- Minced ginger root – 1 tbsp.

Preparation Method:

1. Combine two tablespoons of the cornstarch with the salt and add the beef to coat.
2. Warm up the oil in a wok or deep skillet using the med-hi heat setting.
3. Add the beef and cook for four minutes. Transfer to a bowl.
4. In the same pan, pour one-half cup of the broth and loosen the bits on the bottom. Fold in the broccoli and add one tbsp. of water - if needed. Cook for three minutes with the lid on.
5. Add the garlic, ginger, and pepper flakes. Simmer one more minute.
6. In a mixing cup, combine the rest of the broth, soy sauce, and remainder of the cornstarch. Pour into the pan and lower the temperature setting to med-low. Simmer one more minute and return the juices and beef into the pan. Toss to coat well and serve.

Beef & Mushrooms – Slow Cooker

Freestyle Points: 5

Yields: 6 Servings

Ingredients:

- Lean stewing beef meat – 2 lb.
- Olive oil – 2 tsp.
- Fresh mushrooms – 10 oz.
- Cream of mushroom soup – low-sodium/fat-free – 10.75 oz can
- Soup mix – dry onion – 1 envelope
- Dry red wine - .5 cup
- Suggested Cooker Size: 4-Quarts

Preparation Method:

1. Use the medium heat setting to warm up a skillet.
2. Do the Prep: Cube the stewing beef and slice the mushrooms.
3. Sprinkle the beef with the pepper and salt to your liking. Arrange it in the pan. Layer evenly and brown. Add to the cooker.
4. Brown the mushrooms and toss them into the pot.
5. Stir in the wine and scrape up the browned crunchies. Pour in the soup and soup mix. Mix well and cover.
6. Simmer on low for six to eight hours. Serve when ready.

Jalapeno Popper Burgers

Freestyle Points: 6

Yields: 4 Servings

Ingredients:

- 1 1/3 lb. ground beef – 1.33 lb.
- Finely chopped jalapeno - 1
- Cream cheese - reduced-fat – 2 tbsp.
- Mustard – 2 tsp.
- Worcestershire sauce – 2 tsp.
- Shredded cheddar cheese - .5 cup
- Kosher salt – divided – 5 tsp.

Preparation Method:

1. Combine all of the burger fixings. Divide into six patties and wait about 10 minutes before cooking for the flavors to mix.
2. Grill to your liking (4-6 min. per side suggested). If you prefer, use a skillet and cook for 5-6 minutes for each side.
3. Note: You can also use ground turkey.

Spicy Beef & Zucchini Skillet

Freestyle Points: 6

Yields: 4 Servings

Ingredients:

- Ground beef - lean – 1 lb.
- Olive oil – 1 tsp.
- Minced garlic cloves - 3
- Chopped onion - 1
- Green chilis - 1 can – 4 oz.
- Diced tomatoes - 14 oz. – 2 cans of each
- Drained black beans – 2 cans 14 oz. each
- Lime – juice of 1
- Chili powder – 1 tbsp.
- Chopped zucchinis - 2
- Ground black pepper & Salt – to taste

Preparation Method:

1. Use the med-high setting on the stovetop to heat up the oil.
2. Once it's hot, toss in the onions and garlic. Saute two minutes and add the beef. Once it is browning, stir in the chilis, beans, tomatoes, lime juice, chili powder, pepper, and salt.
3. Continue cooking for 10 minutes. Take off the top and add the chopped zucchini. Cook 10 more minutes and serve.

Fish & Seafood

Apple Trout

Freestyle Points: 3

Yields: 4 Servings

Ingredients:

- Soy sauce – 1 tsp.
- Freshly squeezed lemon juice – 1 tsp.
- Rice vinegar – 1 tsp.
- Granny Smith apple – 1 Medium
- Trout fillets – 7 oz.

Ingredients for the Seasoning Ingredients:

- Black pepper - .5 tsp
- Sea salt - .5 tsp
- Fresh parsley – 1 tbsp.
- Ground dried rosemary - .25 tsp.

Preparation Method:

1. Cut the apple and fillets into bite-sized pieces and squeeze the lemon juice.
2. Whisk the vinegar, lemon juice, soy sauce, rosemary, salt, pepper, and parsley in a mixing dish. Brush the trout.

3. Lightly grease the Instant Pot and add the oil. Using the saute function, add the apple and fish. Prepare 2 minutes. Add enough water to cover and secure the lid.
4. Set the timer for 2 minutes using the high-pressure setting. When the time is completed, open the lid and vent the steam.
5. Serve with your favorite 'zero' veggie.

Cajun Salmon

Freestyle Points: 1

Yields: 4 Servings

Ingredients:

- Olive oil – 1 tbsp.
- Salmon – 1.33 lb.
- Dried thyme - .25 tsp.
- Salt and Pepper - .5 tsp. each
- Paprika – 2 tsp.
- Onion powder - .5 tsp.
- Cayenne - .125 tsp.
- Garlic powder - .5 tsp.

Preparation Method:

1. Combine the spices to make the seasoning.
2. Brush the salmon with oil and a drizzle of the seasoning.
3. On the Grill: Arrange the salmon, so that the skin is facing downwards. Cook three to four minutes. Turn the salmon over and continue cooking for an additional 1-3 minutes. Choose a delicious side dish and serve.

Chapter 5: scrumptious dinner choices: Pork & poultry

Pork

Cuban Pork – Instant Pot

Freestyle Points: 5

Yields: 10 Servings

Ingredients:

- Garlic cloves – 6
- Pork shoulder blade roast – boneless – 3 lb.
- Bay leaf – 1
- Kosher salt – 1 tbsp.
- Lime juice - .66 cup
- Grapefruit juice- .66 cup
- Fresh oregano – 5 tbsp.
- Cumin – 5 tbsp.

Ingredients for Serving:

- Salsa
- Lime wedges
- Chopped cilantro
- Hot sauce
- Tortillas

Preparation Method:

1. Chop the meat into four pieces and place in a mixing container.
2. Use a mini food processor and combine both of the juices, garlic, salt, cumin, and oregano. Blend until smooth.
3. Pour the mixture over the shoulder pieces and let it marinate one hour on the countertop. You can also marinate overnight in the refrigerator.
4. When ready to prepare; add the meat to the cooker along with the bay leaf.
5. Cook using the high-pressure setting for 80 minutes. Natural release the pressure.
6. Shred the meat and remove the juices from the Instant Pot/pressure cooker.
7. Pour one cup of the juices and add the meat back into the pot. Season to taste. Keep it warm until serving time.

Pork Chops with Creamy Sauce

Freestyle Points: 5

Yields: 4 Servings

Ingredients:

- Pork loin chops - center-cut – 4 - Approximately 4 oz. ea.
- Non-fat Half-and-Half - .33 cup
- Fat-free chicken stock - .33 cup
- Black pepper - .5 tsp.
- Onion powder - .5 tsp.
- Salt - .5 tsp.
- Dijon mustard – 1.5 tbsp.
- Dried thyme – 1 pinch

Preparation Method:

1. Shake the salt, pepper, and onion powder over the chops.
2. Using the med-high heat setting on the stovetop, prepare a large skillet with cooking spray.
3. Once the pan is hot, add the chops and fry for 3-4 minutes per side. The internal temperature should reach a minimum temperature on a meat thermometer of 145°F.
4. At this point; just place the prepared chops in a closed container and keep them warm.
5. Pour the chicken stock into the skillet and deglaze the browned bits. Stir in the mustard and Half-and-Half.
6. Lower the temperature setting to medium and continue cooking for 7 minutes. When the sauce has thickened, add the thyme.
7. Serve with the sauce and your favorite side dish.

Raspberry Pork Chops in the Crock Pot

Freestyle Points: 8

Yields: 4 servings

Ingredients:

- Boneless pork chops – 4 – 4 oz. each
- Seasonings: Pepper – salt – meat seasoning; ex. Montreal Steak
- Chicken broth - .25 cup
- Raspberry jam - .75 cup
- Balsamic vinegar – 3 tbsp.
- Chopped chipotle pepper in adobo sauce – 1 tsp.
- Suggested Cooker Size: 4-quarts

Preparation Method:

1. Lightly grease the slow cooker. Whisk the finely chopped chipotle, vinegar, broth, and jam.
2. Season the pork chops to your liking and add two of them to the cooker. Add the sauce and the last two chops with the rest of the sauce.
3. Secure the top and cook 4-6 hours on the low setting.
4. Enjoy with a salad or dish of brown rice.

Poultry

Cheesy Southwestern Chicken – Slow Cooker

Freestyle Points: 1

Yields: 6 Servings

Ingredients:

- Chunky salsa – 16 oz. – 1 jar - divided
- Chicken breast halves - 6
- Corn – 15.5 oz. ea. – 2 cans
- Black beans - 15 oz. – 1 can
- Low-fat shredded Mexican cheese blend – 1 cup
- Optional: Southwest seasoning blend
- Suggested: 5-6-quart slow cooker

Preparation Method:

1. Rinse and drain the corn and black beans. Add to the slow cooker with about half of the salsa.
2. Remove the bones and skin from the chicken. Shake with the salt and pepper or seasoning blend if using.
3. Add the chicken to the pot and the rest of the salsa. Secure the lid and cook on the low-temperature setting until tender (4-6 hrs.).
4. Sprinkle with the cheese. Cover again to melt the cheese (5 min.).

Italian – Balsamic Chicken

Freestyle Points: 1

Yields: 4 Servings

Ingredients:

- Breasts of chicken – 1.33 lb.
- Salt and pepper – 1 tsp. each
- Italian seasoning – 2 tsp.
- Balsamic vinegar – 2.5 tbsp.
- Olive oil – 2 tsp.
- Minced garlic cloves - 3
- Sliced mushrooms - 8 oz.
- Chicken stock - .5 cup

Preparation Method:

1. Combine the salt, pepper, and Italian seasoning. Sprinkle the chicken.
2. Warm up a skillet with the oil using the med-high heat setting. When ready, add the seasoned chicken. Simmer slowly for two to three minutes on each side. Put it to the side for now.
3. Toss the garlic and mushrooms into the pan and saute three to four minutes. Stir in the vinegar and chicken stock. Stir well and deglaze the pan. Toss the chicken in the sauce and simmer about 10 to 15 minutes until done.
4. Note: Be sure to use high-quality balsamic vinegar for the best results.

Oven-Baked Chicken Kebabs – Slow Cooker

Freestyle Points: 2

Yields: 4 Servings

Ingredients:

- Olive oil – 2 tbsp.
- Fresh parsley - .25 cup
- Taco seasoning – 1 tsp.
- Salt – 1 tsp.
- Minced cloves of garlic - 3
- Boneless chicken breasts – 1.33 lb.
- Yellow - red or mixed bell peppers - 2
- Cherry tomatoes – a small handful
- Onion – 1 small
- Juiced limes - 2

Preparation Method:

1. Cut the onion and peppers into chunks. Juice the lime.
2. Add the taco seasoning, salt, garlic, oil, juice of the lime, and parsley in a blender. Process until it's smooth.
3. Cube the chicken and shake in the bag of prepared marinade. Store in the fridge for about 30 minutes.
4. When ready to prepare, warm up the oven broiler.
5. Arrange the chicken tomatoes, peppers, and onions on skewers.
6. Add the prepared kebabs onto a baking tin.

7. Bake for 5 minutes and flip. Broil for another 5 minutes.
8. Serve when the chicken reaches an internal temperature of 165°F.
9. Note: You can add other fixings to the kebabs if you have some extras on hand. (Be sure to check for any additional points.)

Pesto Baked Chicken

Freestyle Points: 3

Yields: 4 Servings

What You Need:

- Butterflied chicken breasts – 1 lb.
- Pesto - .25 cup
- Low-fat grated mozzarella cheese - .5 cup
- Cherry tomatoes- 1 cup
- Sea salt & Freshly cracked black pepper – to your liking

Preparation Method:

1. Cut away all of the bones and skin from the chicken. Slice the tomatoes into halves.
2. Warm up the oven to 400°F. Prepare a baking tin with a sheet of aluminum foil and a spritz of non-stick spray.
3. Coat with the pepper and salt with a spread of the pesto.
4. Place on the baking tin with the tomatoes. Bake 15-17 minutes.
5. Take it out of the oven and drizzle with the cheese. Bake another 5-6 minutes until the cheese is lightly browned.

Chapter 6: Delicious sides

Pair off one of these delicious dishes with your main course.

Sides

Asparagus Sauteed with Bacon

Freestyle Points: 1

Yields: 4 Servings – .66 cup each

Ingredients:

- Medium sliced shallot - 1
- Asparagus – 1 lb.
- Sea salt - .25 tsp.
- Freshly cracked black pepper - .125 tsp.
- Center-cut bacon – 4 slices
- White wine vinegar – 1.5 tsp.

Preparation Method:

6. Slice the bacon into small pieces. Prepare in a skillet for 5 minutes. Remove and drain on a paper towel. Leave only one teaspoon of grease in the pan and pour the rest in a jar for later or discard.
7. Trim and dice the asparagus into chunks and slice the shallots. Add to the pan and saute about 7 minutes, stirring frequently.
8. Toss the bacon, pepper, and salt over the mixture using the med-high temperature until warm.
1. Transfer to serving dishes and stir in the vinegar.

Brown Sugar Baked Beans – Instant Pot

Freestyle Points: 2

Yield: 8 servings

Ingredients:

- Finely diced yellow onion - 1
- Northern beans -approx. 1.75 cups
- Kidney beans - 1 can – 15.5 oz. - approx. 1.75 cups
- Pinto beans - 1 can or approx. 1.75 cups
- Chili powder - 1 tsp.
- Water - .75 cup
- Ketchup - .5 cup
- Dark brown sugar – not packed - .33 cup
- Yellow mustard – 1 tbsp.

Preparation Method:

9. Rinse and drain the beans. Combine all of the fixings in the Instant Pot. Secure the lid and lock. Use the manual setting on high-pressure for 8 minutes.
1. Natural release the pressure when the time has elapsed (10-15 minutes) or quick release if you are in a hurry. Stir before serving.

Caesar Green Beans

Freestyle Points: 2

Yields: 4 Servings

Ingredients for the Beans:

- Water – 2 cups
- Green beans – 1 lb.
- Low-cal Caesar dressing – 1.5 tbsp.
- Shredded parmesan cheese – 1 tbsp.

Ingredients for the Crumb Topping:

- Powdered garlic – 1 tsp.
- Low-cal butter – 1 tsp.
- Whole grain toast – 1 slice

Preparation Method:

1. Trim the green beans and shred the cheese.
2. Toss the greens into a pot of boiling water. Simmer until tender (5 min.). Add to a colander to remove the liquids.
3. Butter the toast and sprinkle with the garlic. Microwave 10 minutes and add to a food processor. Blitz until crumbly.
4. Serve the beans with a sprinkle of the crumbs and a serving of dressing. Sprinkle with the parmesan and serve.

Creamy Broccoli – Instant Pot

Freestyle Points – 4

Yields: 4 Servings

Ingredients:

- Vegetable stock – 2 cups
- Chopped broccoli – 1 lb.
- Halved brussels sprouts – 1 cup
- Sliced red onion – 1 medium-sized
- Minced cloves of garlic – 2
- Salt - .5 tsp.

Ingredients for the Sauce:

- Soy sauce – 1 tbsp.
- Freshly squeezed lime juice – 1 tsp.
- Heavy cream – 2 tbsp.
- Olive oil – 1 tbsp.
- Ground black pepper & salt - .5 tsp. each
- Freshly ground ginger - .25 tsp.
- Also Needed: Food Processor

Preparation Method:

5. Add the brussels sprouts and broccoli to the stainless-steel insert of the Instant Pot. Pour in the vegetable stock and salt.
6. Close the lid and choose the high-pressure setting for five minutes.

7. When the timer buzzes, quick release the pressure and remove the veggies with a slotted spoon.
8. Prep the food processor by adding the garlic, onions, and each of the sauce fixings. Pulse until the mixture is creamy.
9. Select the saute function and pour the prepared sauce into the insert. Let it simmer for five minutes. Stir occasionally.
1. Serve over the veggies and enjoy!

Mashed Sweet Potatoes

Freestyle Points: 2

Servings: 4

Ingredients:

- Large sweet potatoes - 2
- Salt & Black pepper - .5 tsp of each
- Garlic powder – 1 tsp.
- Plain fat-free Greek yogurt - .5 cup

Preparation Method:

1. Wash, peel, and cube the potatoes. Prepare a pot of boiling water (enough to cover the potatoes). Add the potatoes. Boil using the med-high stovetop setting for 8-10 minutes.
2. Dump the potatoes into a colander to drain and add to a large mixing container. Combine with the seasonings and yogurt.
3. Use a hand mixer or mix by hand to mash the fixings until smooth.

Pinto Beans - Crockpot

Freestyle Points: -0-

Yields: 8 Servings

Ingredients:

- Onion - 1
- Dry pinto beans – 1 lb.
- Bay leaves - 2
- Garlic cloves - 4
- Poblano peppers - 2
- Salt – 1 tsp.
- Cumin - .5 tbsp.
- Water or broth – to cover the beans – 6 cups

Preparation Method:

1. Dice the garlic, peppers, and onion. Rinse the beans thoroughly and add to the crockpot.
2. Toss in the rest of the fixings and cover with broth or water. It should be at least one inch over the beans.
3. Prepare for 8-10 hours using the low setting. Times vary with each cooker. When done, the beans will be soft and tasty.

Rainbow Potato Salad

Freestyle Points: 4

Yields: 6 Servings

Ingredients for the Potatoes:

- Yellow potatoes – 1 lb.
- Purple potatoes - .5 lb.
- Red potatoes - .5 lb.

Ingredients for the Dressing:

- Fresh dill - .5 cup
- Scallions - .5 cup
- Celery – 1 stalk
- Low-calorie ranch dressing - .5 cup
- Salt and pepper – to taste

Preparation Method:

1. Cube the potatoes. Finely chop the scallions and celery. Roughly chop the dill.
2. Add all of the potatoes to a pan full of water. Boil and cover. Continue to cook until softened (10-12 min.).
3. Drain the water out of the potatoes and let cool.
4. Combine the dressing fixings in a mixing container. When cool, add the potatoes and stir until incorporated.
5. Chill in the fridge or serve warm.

Roasted Carrots

Freestyle Points: 2

Yields: 4 Servings

Ingredients:

- Baby carrots - 1 bag – 16 oz.
- Dried parsley - .25 tsp.
- Salt - .25 tsp.
- Black pepper – 1 pinch
- Ginger - .25 tsp.
- Cinnamon – 1 pinch
- Olive oil – 1.5 tbsp.
- Also Needed: 9 x 13 casserole dish

Preparation Method:

1. Warm up the oven to 450°F.
2. Prepare the baking dish with the oil and carrots. Sprinkle with the fixings. Bake for 20-25 minutes until tender.
3. Serve with your favorite main dish.

In the next segment, you will discover how easy it is to prepare a days-worth of meals and stay within your desired goals. Once you know how many points you can add to your menu plan (your personal total of allowed points), feel free to add up to those limits and enjoy the freedom provided by your new way of life. Each day has the total provided for points allowed for each recipe item and a daily total.

Chapter 7: 21-day meal plan

DAY 1:
- Breakfast: Baked Omelet – 2
- Lunch: Fish & Shrimp Stew – 2
- Dinner: Beef & Broccoli Stir-Fry – 3

Totals - Day 1: 7

DAY 2:
- Breakfast: Banana Roll-Ups – 2
- Lunch: Buffalo Chicken Tenders – 5
- Lunch Side: Asparagus Sauteed with Bacon – 1
- Dinner: Apple Trout – 3
- Dinner: Side: Brown Sugar Baked Beans – Instant Pot - 2

Totals – Day 2: 13

DAY 3:
- Breakfast: Broccoli Cheddar Egg Muffins - 2
- Lunch: Caesar Salad – Instant Pot – 5
- Dinner: Cheesy Southwestern Chicken – Slow Cooker -1
- Dinner Side: Rainbow Potato Salad – 4

Totals - Day 3: 12

DAY 4:
- Breakfast: Cinnamon-Apple French Toast – 4
- Lunch: Asian Turkey Stir-Fry - 2
- Dinner: Cuban Pork – Instant Pot – 5
- Dinner Side: Pinto Beans – Crockpot - 0-

Totals - Day 4: 11

DAY 5:
- Breakfast: Country Cottage Pancakes – 3
- Lunch: Ham Salad – 2
- Lunch Side: Caesar Green Beans – 2
- Dinner: Beef & Mushrooms – Slow Cooker – 5
- Dinner Side: Roasted Carrots - 2

Totals - Day 5: 14

DAY 6:
- Breakfast: Egg & Sausage Muffins – 1
- Lunch: Pear & Blue Cheese Salad - 3
- Dinner: Cajun Salmon – 1
- Dinner Side: Fully-Loaded Macaroni & Cheese with Veggies – 6

Totals - Day 6: 11

DAY 7:
- Breakfast: Egg & Veggie Scramble - 1
- Lunch: Butternut Squash Soup – 1
- Dinner: Jalapeno Popper Burgers – 6

Totals - Day 7: 8

DAY 8:
- Breakfast: Hard-Boiled Eggs in the Instant Pot -0-
- Lunch: Beef Chili – Slow-Cooker - 4
- Dinner: Italian – Balsamic Chicken – 1
- Dinner Side: Leftover - Dinner Side: Fully-Loaded Macaroni & Cheese with Veggies – 6

Totals - Day 8: 11

DAY 9:
- Breakfast: Tropical Breakfast Pie – 5
- Lunch: Asian Turkey Stir-Fry - 2
- Dinner: Italian – Balsamic Chicken – 1
- Dinner Side: Mashed Sweet Potatoes - 2

Totals - Day 9: 10

DAY 10:
- Breakfast: Muffin Tin Eggs – 1
- Lunch: Chicken-Parmesan Soup – 3
- Dinner: Spicy Beef & Zucchini Skillet - 6

Totals - Day 10: 10

DAY 11:
- Breakfast: Zucchini Noodles & Poached Eggs - 4
- Lunch: Tuna Salad with Cranberries – Onion & Celery - 3
- Dinner: Pork Chops with Creamy Sauce – 5
- Dinner Side: Roasted Carrots - 2

Totals – Day 11: 14

DAY 12:
- Breakfast: Baked Omelet – 2
- Lunch: Lentil Soup – Instant Pot – 1
- Dinner: Oven-Baked Chicken Kebabs – Slow Cooker – 2
- Dinner Side: Asparagus Sauteed with Bacon - 1

Totals - Day 12: 6

DAY 13:

- Breakfast: Egg & Sausage Muffins – 1
- Lunch: Fish & Shrimp Stew - 2
- Dinner: Pork Chops with Creamy Sauce – 5
- Dinner Side: Mashed Sweet Potatoes - 2

Totals - Day 13: 10

DAY 14:

- Breakfast: Broccoli Cheddar Egg Muffins - 2
- Lunch: Ham Salad - 2
- Dinner: Pesto Baked Chicken – 3
- Dinner Side: Creamy Broccoli – Instant Pot - 4

Totals - Day 14: 11

DAY 15:

- Breakfast: Banana Roll-Ups – 2
- Lunch: Vegetable Soup -0-
- Dinner: Raspberry Pork Chops in the Crock Pot – 8
- Dinner Side: Caesar Green Beans - 2

Totals - Day 15: 12

DAY 16:

- Breakfast: Cinnamon-Apple French Toast – 4
- Lunch: Butternut Squash Soup – 1
- Dinner: Apple Trout – 3
- Dinner Side: Brown Sugar Baked Beans – Instant Pot - 2

Totals - Day 16: 10

DAY 17:

- Breakfast: Muffin Tin Eggs – 1
- Lunch: Tuna Salad with Cranberries – Onion & Celery - 3
- Dinner: Beef & Broccoli Stir-Fry – 3

Totals - Day 17: 7

DAY 18:

- Breakfast: Egg & Veggie Scramble - 1
- Lunch: Buffalo Chicken Tenders - 5
- Dinner: Cuban Pork – Instant Pot – 5

Totals - Day 18: 11

DAY 19:

- Breakfast: Breakfast: Hard-Boiled Eggs in the Instant Pot –0-
- Lunch: Pear & Blue Cheese Salad - 3
- Dinner: Spicy Beef & Zucchini Skillet - 6

Totals - Day 19: 9

DAY 20:

- Breakfast: Tropical Breakfast Pie – 5
- Lunch: Beef Chili – Slow-Cooker - 4
- Dinner: Oven-Baked Chicken Kebabs – Slow Cooker – 2
- Dinner Side: Creamy Broccoli – Instant Pot - 4

Totals - Day 20: 15

DAY 21:

- Breakfast: Country Cottage Pancakes - 3
- Lunch: Caesar Salad – Instant Pot – 5

- Dinner: Cajun Salmon – 1
- Dinner Side: Rainbow Side Salad - 4

Totals - Day 21: 13

Now, just continue with the same pattern and add up to your daily number of Freestyle points. These are just your basic meals; so, enjoy the rest of the points but use them wisely each day.

Conclusion

If your lifestyle is so fast-paced that you believe you cannot possibly drag yourself into the kitchen every night of the week and prepare a healthy and nutritious meal; this unique point system is what you have been searching for to assist you in your dieting needs.

It is wise to monitor your points closely while adjusting to the diet plan because there is an 'open window' to overeat. Just remember even though you are eating -0- points, they still contain calories that can add up quickly if you eat too many. Thus, you could put on the pounds and not understand why. It is one of the quirks of the plan, but by following guidelines such as the enclosed 21-day plan; you can enjoy many -0- points.

Now, you have the information, it's time to get busy and prepare a healthy meal without the guilt. Enjoy each deliciously prepared meal!

Index for the recipes

As an additional convenience, as you are preparing your menu; you can use this unique index with the Freestyle points listed for each of the recipe selections.

1: Breakfast Favorites

- Baked Omelet – 2
- Banana Roll-Ups – 2
- Broccoli Cheddar Egg Muffins - 2
- Cinnamon-Apple French Toast – 4
- Country Cottage Pancakes - 3
- Egg & Sausage Muffins – 1
- Egg & Veggie Scramble - 1
- Hard-Boiled Eggs in the Instant Pot -0-
- Muffin Tin Eggs – 1
- Tropical Breakfast Pie – 5
- Zucchini Noodles & Poached Eggs

2: Lunch Favourites

Poultry

- Asian Turkey Stir-Fry - 2
- Buffalo Chicken Tenders - 5

Salads

- Caesar Salad – Instant Pot – 5
- Ham Salad - 2
- Pear & Blue Cheese Salad - 3
- Tuna Salad with Cranberries – Onion & Celery – 3

Soups

- Beef Chili – Slow-Cooker - 4
- Butternut Squash Soup – 1
- Chicken-Parmesan Soup – 3
- Fish & Shrimp Stew - 2
- Lentil Soup – Instant Pot – 1
- Vegetable Soup -0-

3: scrumptious dinner choices: Beef – fish & seafood

Beef Choices

- Beef & Broccoli Stir-Fry – 3
- Beef & Mushrooms – Slow Cooker – 5
- Jalapeno Popper Burgers – 6
- Spicy Beef & Zucchini Skillet - 6
- Fish & Seafood
- Apple Trout – 3
- Cajun Salmon - 1

4: scrumptious dinner choices: Pork & poultry

Pork

- Cuban Pork – Instant Pot – 5
- Pork Chops with Creamy Sauce – 5
- Raspberry Pork Chops in the Crock Pot - 8

Poultry

- Cheesy Southwestern Chicken – Slow Cooker -1
- Italian – Balsamic Chicken – 1

- Oven-Baked Chicken Kebabs – Slow Cooker - 2
- Pesto Baked Chicken – 3

5: Sides

- Asparagus Sauteed with Bacon – 1
- Brown Sugar Baked Beans – Instant Pot - 2
- Caesar Green Beans – 2
- Creamy Broccoli – Instant Pot - 4
- Fully-Loaded Macaroni & Cheese with Veggies – 6
- Mashed Sweet Potatoes – 2
- Pinto Beans – Crockpot - 0-
- Rainbow Potato Salad – 4
- Roasted Carrots -

PART 2

INTRODUCTION

Acid reflux is one of the most common ailments affecting adults today. This is due to the notion that there are so many contributing factors and catalysts that can spawn its symptoms. As a result, educating oneself on the best ways to care for the symptoms of reflux is paramount for avoiding and overcoming them once they arise.

Evidently, a common refrain for most reflux sufferers is to avoid foods and drinks that are spicy and or fizzy. While these are certainly helpful approaches to take, you are well advised to consider approaches such as increased exercise for maintenance of overall health, avoiding certain exercises altogether if you are already suffering from severe GERD, implementing dietary changes such as limiting coffee intake, cutting back on peppermint and avoiding highly acidic foods.

But acid reflux symptoms are not caused solely by poor dietary choices alone. Indeed, smoking in excess and excess alcohol consumption are also consistent contributing factors that can induce acid reflux symptoms leading to GERD and Barrett's disease. Leveraging the knowledge presented in this book with regard to the specific dietary and lifestyle changes you must implement, along with acquiring a deeper understanding of the particular scientific reasons for acid reflux, will allow for an informed perspective so that your approach to the symptoms presented is equipped with the most up-to-date and effectual information.

When equipped with these strategies and general knowledge concerning acid reflux, you will certainly be at a distinct advantage when you are confronted by the painstaking and, at its most extreme, life-threatening, symptoms of acid reflux.

Chapter 1: Chronic Acid Reflux & Its Serious health Implications

Acid reflux is the result of abundant backflow of acid for your stomach into the esophagus. Anatomically, when your lower esophageal sphincter (LES) becomes weakened by, among many causal factors, continually consuming a high diet, acid can flow back into your esophagus causing acid reflux. Consequently, there are numerous symptoms that are spawned by acid reflux including, most notoriously, heartburn and indigestion. While high acidity in the gut is common for everybody and is often devoid of serious health concerns if occurring on a minimal basis, serious health concerns can develop if high acidity can persist for a prolonged period of time. If left unattended and without measures of control put in place, in many instances, these health issues will lead to hospitalization or even death.

In the most serious cases, chronic long-term heartburn, known as Gastroesophageal Reflux Disease (GERD), Barett's esophagus and esophageal problems can arise due to uncontrolled and unaddressed chronic acidity. Some of these most serious ailments are the remnants of years of neglecting the symptoms of acid reflux, particularly after big meals. Over time, the backflow of acid from your stomach damages your esophagus causing erosion of the layers lining the walls of the organ. This inflammation often leads to very painful swelling in esophagus called esophagitis and is accompanied by a painful swallowing feeling. In addition, esophageal ulcers are the most common ailment of an inflamed esophagus. In fact, GERD is the main cause of these ulcers in the lining of the esophagus. Moreover, painful swallowing, nausea, chest pain contribute to a lack of sleep which perpetuates many of these symptoms simplify virtue of that fact that your body is not getting the required rest to overcome these symptoms. As soon as these symptoms arise, be sure to consult a doctor too so that you can be prescribed medication to treat the symptoms before they grow into more serious, persistent conditions. Acquiring medial intervention is especially important when dealing with an ulcer; indeed, ulcers are extremely harmful to the lining of your organ and can be incredibly persistent if left unattended and given time to grow.

Even more, if your highly acidic diet remains the same as before the ulcer, this contributing factor will only enhance the growth of your ulcer and some of your other symptoms. Over time, the scarring of the lining within your esophagus will lead to scar tissue build up, thereby narrowing the esophagus altogether. Swallowing food and drinks will be made much more difficult as a result and may require a surgical procedure to expand the esophagus. These narrow areas of your esophagus are called strictures, and will likely lead to dangerous weight loss and or dehydration. Avoiding a procedure through immediate medical treatment of high acidity is clearly the preferred approach; but once these strictures block your esophageal pathways, a surgical procedure will be required.

Another common ailment of high acidity that affects many people is Barret's esophagus. Specifically, around 10%-15 of people who suffer from GERD will begin to also develop this painful condition, which results in dangerous changes in cells due to excess stomach acid. Thankfully, less than 1% of those who suffer from Barret's esophagus will actually develop esophageal cancer. If intervened early enough in the process, doctors are able to remove any of these abnormally developed cells through a procedure known as an endoscopy, whereby doctors will insert a flexible tube accompanied by a small camera into your esophagus. However, those who have GERD are at a, albeit slightly, increased risk of developing esophageal cancer. Even still, be sure to consult a doctor as soon as your symptoms reach a persistently painful level so that proactive measures and treatment can be implemented to quell your pain, and inhibit the growth of cancer cells.

If there is a long history of esophageal cancer in your family, you will be at an increased risk of developing this cancer as well, especially if you attain medical treatment after a prolonged period of time experiencing symptoms of high acidity. If you are aware of having a family history of esophageal cancer, make sure to ask your doctor for a regular endoscopy to find and mitigate the growth of improper cells. Moreover, tooth decay is a very common symptom of excess stomach acid as it wears down the outer layer of your teeth (enamel). As a result, this can lead to excess cavities and weakened teeth. In a recent study, researchers found that over 40% of GERD patients showed significant tooth decay, along with 70% of patients whose reflux had managed to reach the upper esophagus), compared to only 10% of those patients that had no symptoms of reflux. Certainly, reading about the symptoms that accompany stomach acid is disconcerting and worrisome. Nonetheless, being aware of the symptoms and knowing the early signs of their emergence will mitigate the risks of cancer and other chronic ailments like GERD and Barret's esophagus.

So, what can you do about these symptoms and potentially life-altering health concerns if you are experiencing excess stomach acid? Initially, and rather obviously, begin by assessing your diet. If you typically consume large meals, cut down your portions by at least 25%, and avoid eating right before you sleep. The latter is especially important for your digestive track as your body has to work harder to digest food whilst you are asleep and when your body's organs are supposed to be at rest. Also, limit your chocolate and coffee intake. Typically, medical professionals recommend limiting your coffee intake to only 2-3 cups per day at the most. If these levels are exceeded, your body's acidity levels will climb to healthy proportions and heighten your likelihood of acquiring the aforementioned symptoms. In the same way, excess consumption of alcohol and peppermint carry very harmful side-effects. Not mention, smoking is by far the most dangerous to many of your body's organs, especially the esophagus. Taking steps to cut back and eventually quit smoking is strongly recommended to not only avoid esophageal cancer and weakened tooth enamel, but for a bevy of other health-related reasons not directly associated with stomach acidity. When consulting a doctor to address stomach acid symptoms, you will most likely be prescribed an antacid, H2 blocker or a proton pump inhibitor (PPI); all three are available by prescription as well as over the counter.

Where GERD is concerned, there are other major factors that you should look out for. These symptoms are not specific to a particular body type or even certain foods. First, heartburn is, as mentioned, a clear indicator of GERD and is usually an only an occasional issue that is known to affect over 60 million people at least once or twice a month on average. However, for the 20 million individuals who suffer from heartburn on a chronic level through GERD, seemingly unrelated symptoms can inevitably result in numerous other health complications. You are well advised to consult a doctor if you find that you suffer frequent heartburn (two-three times per week regularly).

When you suffer from GERD, acid, food, as well as digestive juices tend to flow back into your esophagus from the pit of your stomach. Over time, this results in esophagitis, thereby leaving the king of the walls of the esophagus extremely vulnerable to additional harm through scarring, tearing and even deterioration. Additionally, while the primary symptom of GERD is heartburn, there are likely to be other symptoms that are far more difficult to diagnose for doctors and patients alike. Notably, doctors refer to a symptom known as, "silent reflux," which includes voice changes, chronic coughing, major and prolonged throat soreness, along with hoarseness. Patients may have a sustained sensation of having a lump in their throatier having the constant urge for having to clear one's throat. Another common symptom of GERD is the effect that stomach acid has on your breathing. Indeed, GERD, for instance, can heighten the extreme effects of asthma and or pneumonia. Whether or not patients have a history of lung problems personally or with regard to their family lineage, GERD can cause difficulty in breathing and persistent shortness of breath. However, treating this particular symptom is especially tricky; according to several recent studies, GERD medication, like PPIs, have been shown to increase pneumonia by directly contributing to the growth of harmful bacteria. Also, researchers have found that many prescribed PPIs suppress coughing that is needed to clear the lungs. As a result, your doctor may be forced to consider the function of your lungs when prescribing PPIs when in the process of treating symptoms associated with acid reflux.

Many people with ulcers from acid reflux tend to spit up blood and or see it in their stool. For a point of clarity, be sure to note that Esophageal ulcers are much different than stomach ulcers as they (stomach) are usually due to bacteria. Blood from esophageal ulcers, however, tend to be red or a darker purple-red color. If you find yourself having such symptoms, be sure to contact your doctor immediately. The immediate response from your doctor will likely be a schedules endoscopy mentioned earlier. In addition, you may also be prescribed acid-blocking or acid-reducing meds can treat these dangerous stomach ulcer.

An overarching common symptom of acid reflux is a lower quality of life. According to a 2004 study from Europe, whereby 6,000 GERD patients reported that their quality of life had been significantly diminished due to problems that are associated with drink, food and sleep, along with social and physical limitations. Not to mention, there can be major financial implications from having to buy an abundant amount of medications to treat the myriad symptoms of acid reflux, as well as the possible surgical procedures and endoscopy sessions that may be needed if the symptoms escalate to advanced stages. Moreover, the quality of life for patients of GERD was strikingly similar to heart-attack patients and was even lower, in certain cases, for those patients struggling with diabetes and cancer.

Generally, the healing time-frame for GERD is around 2 to 8 weeks. If allowed to persist without medicinal intervention, symptoms of GERD can inflict a considerable amount of damage. For example, reflux esophagitis (RO) can create visible and painful cracks and breaks in the esophageal mucosa. In order to fully and effectively heal RO, acid suppression for a prolonged period (roughly 3-9 weeks) is required and will likely be the timeframe advised by your doctor. Keep in mind that healing rates will rapidly improve as acid suppression increases.

Chronic stress is also a significant factor in the development, growth and persistence of acid reflux. Our digestive system, moreover, is intricately associated with our nervous system. When stress presents itself, especially in an overwhelming or uncontrollable manner, our digestive system will then receive a lower amount of blood flow, thus causing various issues. Further, our gut bacteria are implicated in our management of stress at increasing levels, so probiotics are helpful in helping the management of this development.

Chapter 2: The role of Fibre, Prebiotics and Probiotics

Incorporating key changes into your diet can carry massive benefits with regard to dealing with the many symptoms of acid reflux. Specifically, consuming more fiber is an excellent way to mitigate the harsh symptoms. An important point of clarity is the distinction between dietary fiber, defined as edible but non-digestible carbohydrate-based material, and insoluble fiber. Dietary fiber is mainly available in abundance naturally in many cereals, grains, plants, and vegetables as these all play a major role in gastrointestinal health. Given the importance of fiber, and its positive impact in easing the symptoms of acid reflux, many people on average are dangerously deficient in fiber. This deficiency includes both the soluble and insoluble forms of fiber. The main difference between these two forms of fiber are found in their role in digestion; insoluble fiber expedites the travel of foods through the gastrointestinal tract, while solute fibers have been shown to slow the digestion process.

While the varied and, at times, monotonous science concerning acid reflux is still in progress and remains to be settled. Nevertheless, the theoretical benefits of adequate intake of fiber include avoiding trigger foods altogether, as well as the stomach-filling "full" effect of fiber and fewer relaxation reactions of the anti-reflux valve residing between the stomach and the esophagus. Even still, there exists a persistent relationship between acid reflux trigger and the role of fiber. To elaborate, soluble fiber has been shown to induce the body to draw fluid out of already digested food, which then contributes added bulk to your meals which leaves you with a feeling of being "full" for a far more prolonged period of time. As it is commonly found within such sources as barley, peas as well as oat bran, soluble fiber does play an active role in regulating glucose levels and may even contribute to signaling the brain that the stomach is in fact full both during and after eating a meal of any size. Moreover, smaller meals can help acid reflux by refraining from overfilling your stomach. Whereas, insoluble fiber as found within vegetables and whole grains can speed up the passage of stomach contents to your intestinal tract, thereby decreasing your body's propensity for reflux.

Additionally, fatty, fried foods are typically much lower in fiber and are also frequently accompanied by the triggering symptoms of regurgitation, indigestion, and heartburn. Indeed, a fiber-rich diet like fresh fruits, vegetables, and whole-grain bread can tend to contribute to fewer instances of reflux symptoms arising. Some dietary fibers are also widely considered to be probiotics. Note the key distinction between prebiotics and probiotics: the latter refers to the specific helpful bacteria itself, with prebiotic referring to bacterial nutrients. In other words, prebiotics are nutrients which are left for bacteria to digest, or, more plainly, fuel to encourage the balanced bacterial growth within digestive organs. Here, the role of fiber in greatly improving the many symptoms of acid reflux is illuminated; this role is as a bacterial intermediary. On the whole, nonetheless, particular items in your diet tend to perform a seemingly minor role in the symptoms associated with acid reflux. Those who suffer from chronic acid reflux are strongly advised to avoid those specific foods that can aggravate painful heartburn and regurgitation; however, eliminating a broad range of food from your diet is no recommended as it can detrimental to your overall health. Instead, you should note foods and beverages that can trigger acid reflux specifically and root them out from your diet as soon as possible.

There is a tremendous amount of evidence in favor of incorporating a fiber-rich diet into your daily routine. Notably, the benefits are particular to the overall maintenance of your gut and with regard to managing the amount of harmful bacteria native to that region of your body. A study from 2004 that involved over 65,000 people revealed that fiber intake was associated with the improved perception of acid reflux symptoms. Also, this study revealed people who consumed high fiber bread were nearly three times as likely to experience relief of acid reflux symptoms compared to people who consumed bread with lower fiber content. Granted, the reasons for these results remains unknown; however, the authors of the broad study have speculated that the digestive process of fiber can also be a catalyst for enhanced muscle relaxation from the stomach through the esophagus as it tightens the anti-reflux valve.

So, what are the disadvantages of fiber in acid reflux? It is true that fiber is especially helpful when serving to ease acid reflux symptoms, excess fiber consumption has been shown to aggravate the symptoms. A study published in a medical journalism 2014 indicated that consuming a minimum of 10 grams of highly fermentable starches each day can significantly contribute to painful episodes of acid reflux symptoms. An additional study noted that nine participants who were diagnosed with GERD, those patients who consumed a prebiotic known as fructooligo also had elevated instances of acid reflux symptoms than those patients who were given a placebo.

There are many aspects to consider when striving to efficiently manage acid reflux symptoms. Among them, dietary fiber is perhaps the most important or, at the very least, the most consequential. For instance, while being excessively overweight is certainly risk factor as far as GERD is concerned, adequate consumption of healthy fiber will aid in keeping the weight at a healthy level. Excess fiber, however, causes stomach distension in may people, along with enhanced stomach pressure as well as prolonged emptying on the stomach in many cases, all of which have shown to lead to accentuated acid reflux symptoms. Medical professionals specializing in gastroenterology strongly recommend implementing lifestyle changes such as eating smaller sized meals on a frequent basis (as opposed to larger meals a few times per day), limiting overall consumption of carbonated beverages and foods high in salt content with the intent of improving the acid reflux symptoms. Note that women over the age of 50 should try to consume 25 grams per day; on the other hand, men under 50 are strongly advised to consume 38 grams of fiber each day. While consuming more laxatives is often the approach undertaken by people dealing with symptoms of acid reflux, medical professionals advise increasing your fiber content within your diet for maximized results, as well as maintaining your overall health as laxatives can take a substantial toll on your body and its digestive tract. Consuming a higher amount of fiber will strengthen your stool, keep wastes traveling more smoothly through your intestinal tract, along with preventing constipation. During this process of consuming more fibre, be sure to also ensure that you are consuming plenty of water as well; for fiber to have its absolute best effect, it is imperative that your body remain as hydrated as possible to make sure that waste moves smoothly along your intestinal tract rather than building up due to rigidity.

A good source of probiotics and fiber is yogurt, which carries "good" bacteria helpful for overall maintenance of gut health. A healthy gut is paramount for an efficient and well-functioning intestinal tract and digestive system. Prebiotics and probiotics are, essentially, analogous to food for the bacteria in your stomach; bananas, corn, and whole wheat are additional food sources that are high in prebiotics. Moreover, one of the most beneficial aspects of a fiber-rich diet is the notion that high-fiber foods help control your cravings for snacks. Certainly, high fiber diets can help you lose weight as it displaces other calories for overall maintenance of health.

Guarding against illness, fiber-rich diets will also lower your chances of developing major gut-related illnesses such as diverticulitis. This condition, pockets in the walls of colon trap waste as opposed to moving it along. While doctors remain unsure of the direct catalyst(s) for the illness, consuming a high-fiber diet moves waste fervently along through your system. Along with diverticulitis, a high-fiber diet also eases and prevents irritable bowel syndrome— which has also been linked to acid reflux, albeit a rarer, more extreme symptom. Nevertheless, the most common symptom of acid reflux— heartburn— is quelled by a fiber-rich diet.

Probiotics are becoming increasingly linked to the management of the symptoms associated with acid reflux and alleviating these issues. For a more technical explanation, as we are already aware that probiotics are an effective way of balancing the gut bacteria inside of our bodies, they also help combat against a bacterial infection knows as, H. pylori. This bacterial infection usually originates in childhood. This bacteria, found in the stomach, can alter the environment around them through reducing the acidity levels so that they can survive for longer periods of time. By penetrating the lining of the stomach, thereby remaining hidden and protected by the mucous membrane so that the body's immune defenses cannot reach them. In addition, these bacteria tend to secrete an enzyme called urease, which converts urea to ammonia. The presence of ammonia in this instance is significant because it reduces the stomach acidity around the specific area where the bacteria is found. Coincidentally, it is this lower stomach acid that is often mistaken— by doctors and patients alike— for acid reflux. Can probiotics help combat H. pylori? Well, many medical researchers believe that probiotics can, in fact, help battle this bacteria in several key ways. For one, probiotics are believed to strengthen the protective barrier against H. pylori by producing antimicrobial substances, along with competing against H. pylori for what is known as adhesion receptors (space on the lining of the stomach). Also, it is believed that probiotics assist in stabilizing the gut's mucosal barrier. Many researchers even argue that the production of relatively large amounts of lactate is another inhibitory factor of H. pylori due to the possibility that it could lower the H. pylori urease. Not to mention, probiotics may also be effective in modifying inflammation levels by interacting with the epithelial cells that are responsible for managing the secretion of inflammatory proteins in the gut.

Depending on the particular cause of your acid reflux, probiotics can be incredibly useful for alleviating the painful symptoms. Probiotics can be taken in conjunction with an antacid without worry of the antacid overtaking the positive benefits of the probiotic. More importantly, your approach should be to uncover the root of your acid reflux and adjust medical intervention accordingly. Of course, you doctor plays a huge role in this process, especially in diagnosing the specific cause of your acid reflux; still, it is your responsibility to seek medical expertise so that you can tackle the root of the symptoms as opposed to addressing the individual symptoms as they arise. Being aware of the triggers in both the food and drinks that you consume, managing your stress levels regardless of how often they fluctuate, and finding the specific levels of acid within your stomach are critical steps to address the symptoms of acid reflux. More likely than not, the best method of dealing with your symptoms will be to implement a diverse approach that incorporates a range of approaches rather than relying solely on medical intervention.

Chapter 3: Understanding the role of proteins, carbs, AND fats in healing acid damage

In recent years, there have been increasing reports concerning the benefits of a low-carb diet in healing the damage induced by acid damage. This may seem counterintuitive given the notion that the standard treatment for GERD includes the *removal* of certain foods that increase acidity in the stomach, for example, tomato sauces which are believed to be contributing causes of excess stomach acidity. Also, as mentioned in chapter 1, the removal of coffee, alcohol, smoking, and peppermint are other dietary and lifestyle changes that ease GERD symptoms. Additionally, researchers have found that diets with a higher amount of carbohydrates can significantly elevate symptoms of acid reflux. Whereas, a low-carb diet has also been shown to reduce symptoms of GERD. While many health researchers and medical experts have expressed concern over the exceptionally low proportion of daily calories from fat and protein in low-carb diets, as wells calorie levels being considerably lower in these diet than recommended. Nevertheless, the effects of gastroesophageal reflux disease have been shown to be significantly reduced after implementation of a low-carb diet. For a case in point, following a 2001 research study in which 5 individuals with diverse ranges of GERD symptoms and across the age spectrum, engaged in a low-carb diet, each of the 5 research participants showed significant relief of symptoms. Granted, throughout the duration of the study, which spanned 8 months, 3 of the 5 research participants also reduced their coffee intake concurrently.

The concurrent reduction of coffee, coupled with lower intake of carbohydrates, was shown to be effective in reducing symptoms such as heartburn and stomach pain. Interestingly, while coffee reduction was a contributing factor, observations from a few of the participants revealed that exacerbating foods such as coffee and fat are less pertinent when a low-carb diet is strictly followed. In other words, when implementing a low-carb diet, the effects of classic factors like coffee and fat intake are vastly diminished even if their consumption is not significantly reduced. So, whether or not you choose to reduce coffee and fat intake significantly, you are likely to reduce most GERD symptoms by solely undertaking a low-carb diet. Therefore, the logical conclusion to draw from these findings is that a low-carb diet is a significant factor for reducing the symptoms of acid reflux. This conclusion gains even more credibility when considering the propensity for high-carb diets to aggravate GERD symptoms.

In addition to lower carbohydrates, lean sources of protein and healthy fats are beneficial for reducing symptoms associated with acid reflux. Lean proteins found in eggs are a great addition to your diet for reducing acid reflux symptoms; however, they are a problem for many people due to elevated cholesterol. If eggs are an issue for you, be sure to consume only egg whites and refrain for consuming higher fat yolks—which have been shown to elevate GERD symptoms. Moreover, as high-fat meals and fried food typically descries LES pressure thereby delaying emptying of the stomach and boosting the risk of acid reflux, it is in your best interest to choose lean grilled meats, as well as poached, baked or broiled meats. Boosting proteins, in the way, will also provide benefits for your overall health as well. Also, complex carbohydrates, as found in rice, whole grain bread, couscous and oatmeal carry excellent benefits for reducing GERD symptoms and easing any scarring that may already be present in the walls of your esophagus. Specifically, brown rice and whole grains add valuable fiber your diet. Root vegetables such as potatoes are excellent sources of healthy carbohydrates and easily digestible fiber. Remember to refrain from incorporating too much garlic and onion while preparing your meals, which are can commonly irritate the esophagus and stomach lining. Along with proteins and complex carbs, incorporating healthy fats has great benefits for easing GERD symptoms and other symptoms accompanying acid reflux. A type of nutrient, fat is high in calories but certainly a necessary component of your diet. Keep in mind, however, fats can vary and they do not all have the same effect on your body. On the whole, you are well advised to avoid consuming a high amount of saturated fats as typically found in dairy and meat, along with trans fats found in processed foods, shortening and margarine. As a replacement, unsaturated fats from fish and or plants are recommended; some examples of monounsaturated fats include sesame, olive, canola, sunflower, peanuts, seeds and nuts, as well as butter. In addition, examples of polyunsaturated fats include such oils as safflower, corn, flaxseed and walnut, fatty fish such as salmon and trout, along with soybean.

Some other helpful tips for reducing acid reflux symptoms include chewing gum, as long as it is not spearmint- or peppermint-flavored. Chewing gum increases the amount of saliva production in your mouth and also reduces the amount of acid in your esophagus. While alcohol consumption has already been mentioned in earlier chapters, research suggests that some people begin to experience extreme symptoms after only one drink; if you fall into this category, be sure to experiment with your levels to uncover what amount is best for you. Additionally, during and after each meal, particularly bigger meals, be sure to remain aware of your posture. Generally, it is a good idea to sit up while you are eating and avoid lying flat on your back for at least hours post-meal. Standing up and walking around the room after a big meal can help encourage the flow of gastric juices in the right direction. Further, avoiding eating big meals before bed can help you refrain from overloading your digestive system while you sleep. Digestion increases the overall amount of gastric acid that is present within your stomach. When laying down, LES's ability to inhibit stomach contents from traveling through the esophagus decreases significantly. When operating concurrently, excess stomach acid and remaining in a reclined position for an unexpended period of time create an abundance of acid reflux symptoms. On the whole, consuming a large meal for less than 3 to 4 hours prior to bed is generally not advisable for those suffering from persistent GERD symptoms; however, the timing of these symptoms can certainly vary depending on the individual.

In a 2017 research study on the benefits of healthy dietary changes versus drug intervention, researchers studied the effects of dietary changes to a type of reflux known as laryngopharyngeal reflux or LPR. This reflux is essentially triggered when pepsin, a digestive enzyme from the stomach, reaches the sensitive tissues in the upper section of the digestive tract. Symptoms like throat clearing and hoarseness are common with pepsin in the throat and or upper part of the digestive tract. In the study, the researchers had participants suffering from acid reflux switch to a Mediterranean diet and consuming significantly more water, thereby neutralizing excess acid. In this particular study, participants avoided classic triggers such as coffee, peppermint, alcohol, fatty and spicy foods, chocolate and soda. Another set of participants were given pharmaceutical drugs to ease GERD symptoms.

After a six week timeframe, participants of the study reported a greater percent of declines in their GERD symptoms as those participants that had used drugs to address the symptoms. Granted, the study did not elaborate on the particular ways in which that the diet and increased water consumption eased the symptoms; nonetheless, the Mediterranean diet incorporates eating mostly plant-based fruits and vegetables. In addition, the increased water can mitigate pepsin's acidity levels in the throat. As mentioned, fruits, vegetables and water are great methods of reducing acid reflux and GERD symptoms. With this in mind, the positive benefits experienced by the study's participants is not surprising in the least.

Adjusting your diet for GERD does not require removing all of the foods that you typically enjoy eating. Instead, a few simple changes to your diet if more than enough to address the uncomfortable symptoms of GERD. Your aim in addressing the GERD symptoms should be to create a well-rounded, nutrient-based diet that incorporates a variety of foods that include vegetables, fruits, complex carbs, healthy fats and lean sources of protein. Healing acid reflux damage is made significantly easier when starting with dietary changes that add healthy and diverse foods. Coupled with medical intervention (if required), healthy dietary changes can carry great benefits for healing scarring in your esophagus and stomach, as well as symptoms such as heartburn, bloating and even tooth decay.

Chapter 4: Exercise to reduce acid reflux

When GERD symptoms escalate and you are still in the early stages of implementing dietary changes to address acid reflux symptoms, exercise can be a great option for reducing the symptoms. When GERD symptoms begin to arise, high-impact physical activities like running, skipping rope and jumping exercises. If you are overweight or obese, a weight loss of 10% has been shown to reduce GERD symptoms like heartburn, bloating and reflux. A self-reported analysis study of individuals experiencing GERD symptoms fund that those who reduced their Body Mass Index (BMI) by 2 kilograms or 4.4 pounds or more, along with the circumference of their waist by 5cm or more has improved their GERD symptoms significantly. In contrast, there are also certain exercises that can induce reflux by opening the lower esophageal sphincter (LES) during workouts such as heavy lifting, stomach crunches, or other high impact exercises. When the LES opens, stomach acid travels up into the esophagus causing heartburn.

There are some common sense tips concerning exercise for managing GERD symptoms. First, this twice about how much and what you are eating prior to starting your exercise routine. Obviously, less food in your stomach is ideal. If you are too full, you should wait at least 1 to 2 hours before initiating your exercise routine. This will allow for food to pass fro your stomach through to the small intestine. With less food in your stomach while exercising, it is significantly less likely that you will experience the painful and annoying symptoms of acid reflux such as heartburn and bloating. Next, you should choose the food you consume with thought and, in some instances, caution. Generally, you should avoid foods that trigger GERD symptoms (choosing complex carbohydrates is advised). Your stomach does metabolize these foods much faster than others through a process known as gastric emptying. Moreover, diabetics should avoid high fat and high protein foods before exercise due to being more susceptible to experiencing slow gastric emptying. Experts also suggest adjusting your workout if you suffer from frequent GERD symptoms. Starting at a slower pace with workouts that put less strain on your body like controlled walking and controlled weight training in either a sitting or standing position is strongly recommended. Whereas, high impact, high-intensity workouts like running, rowing and cycling and induce acid reflux. Additionally, acrobatic workouts and gymnastics can also disrupt stomach contents. The key is to avoid exercises that jostle the LES and reflux, these are typically positions that put your body in awkward positions like being upside down defying gravity in one way or another.

A great exercise that carries tremendous benefits for improving and relieving acid reflux symptoms and digestion is yoga. One particular study from 2014 found that six months of yoga significantly reduced acid reflux and stomach bloating, along with improved esophagitis. Again, however, try to avoid positions that heighten GERD symptoms. If any of these "lifestyle" changes fail to improve your GERD symptoms during exercise, be sure to consult your doctor about being prescribed medication for acid-suppression. And, of course, engaging in a constant exercise routine is not only very beneficial with regard to improving your GERD symptoms, but also for the maintenance of your overall health.

Chapter 5: How to live a reflux free life?

As you may have already noticed, acid reflex can be induced by an abundance of factors ranging from diet, bad habits, poor sleep hygiene, and many other factors. Clearly, it isn't just as simple as cutting out bad habits and instilling a series of great dietary and lifestyle changes. But whether you are able to successfully implement these changes or not does not, thankfully, hinge on strict adherence to a stringent diet or eliminating some of your favorite guilty habits. But before you can begin to consider stepping into a reflux-free life, you should be cognizant of the stages of reflux and recovery.

Firstly, almost everyone who suffers from GERD begins with normal LES and little to no reflux. The severity level of GERD, therefore, more than likely correlates to best with the overall degree of damage inflicted upon the sphincter. Note, however, that this is not easy to determine. Normally, the amount of damage to your sphincter correlates with the overall severity of acid reflux symptoms. This severity is most often determined by the volume, frequency, and duration of reflux episodes. In turn, these factors will correlate with GERD symptoms such as regurgitation and heartburn. If you are diagnosed with GERD, your strategy for addressing the symptoms and eventually overcoming them should first be to containment. Unfortunately, damage to your LES caused by GERD cannot be reversed by drugs and is permanent. Nonetheless, many patients of GERD have been able to live with these symptoms and with functionality despite damage to the sphincter. Changing simple lifestyle habits, such as sleeping and eating, can significantly decrease and prevent severe reflux episodes in spite of damage to your sphincter. In Stage 1 of GERD, known as Mild GERD, most adults currently have minimal damage to their LES and tend to experience mild GERD occasionally. Most often, the adults are left with either tolerating occasional heartburn or will have to use over-the-counter acid suppressive medications from the onset of symptoms through its subsequent stages. Typically, when taking drugs to address the symptoms, quality of life for patients is not affected because the medications are very effective in suppressing symptoms. If you choose to take medication to address symptoms, make sure that you are also cleaning up your diet. If you continue to consume trigger foods and beverages, like coffee and certain sauces, for example, the benefits you garner from medication will be minimal and your recovery will be prolonged if not inhibited altogether. Replacing these meals with smaller, leaner meals that do not pose a threat to inducing symptoms of GERD is recommended. This will ease heartburn and lessen the damage to your sphincter.

In stage 2, known as Moderate GERD, symptoms are far more difficult to control and use of prescribed acid-suppressive drugs will be needed. In this stage, reflux is accompanied by symptoms that are far more intense than stage 1. Therefore, medicinal intervention is needed to mitigate the damage and pain caused by these symptoms. Still, many symptoms in this stage can be managed by using acid-suppressive drugs for prolonged periods of time. Keep in mind that over-the-counter medication can provide insufficient relief; whereas, prescription strength medications are needed in order for you to manage GERD symptoms effectively. Additionally, stage 3, or, Severe GERD, can result in a very low quality if life and is generally considered to be an extremely serious problem by medical professionals specializing in GERD. Because prescription grade acid-suppressive drugs and medicinal intervention usually do not control symptoms, regurgitation is frequent. In Stage 3, it is entirely possible that complications associated with erosive GERD are present. Lastly, stage 4, or, reflux-induced esophageal cancer, is quite obviously the most serious stage. The result of numerous years of severe reflux, nearly 16% of all long-term reflux sufferers progress to this extremely advanced stage. Due to the long-term reflux, the esophagus' lining has been heavily damaged, thereby resulting in a high degree of cellular changes. Also, stage 4 is the stage that involves the pre-cancerous condition called Barrett's esophagus and or an even more severe condition called dysplasia. Granted, these conditions are not cancerous. However, they are capable of raising the risk of developing reflux-induced esophageal cancer. Accordingly, at this stage, common GERD symptoms are likely to also be accompanied by a strong burning sensation in the throat, chronic coughing, and persistent hoarseness. A narrowing of the esophagus, or strictures, will also be present in this stage, and can also be characterized by the sensation that food is sticking to your throat. However, this is only a feeling associated with strictures. Notably, this symptom is also caused by esophageal cancer. Keep in mind that stage 4 GERD can only be diagnosed by a medical professional through an endoscopy and from an intrusive biopsy of cells retrieved from the lower esophagus.

A 30-day recovery plan for GERD symptom can be easily broken into weekly steps. In the first week, you will presumably be trying to lean off of the medication that you have been prescribed. A reversion plan of this nature should take into account a variety of approaches that incorporate dietary changes, exercise routines, sleep schedules, and other lifestyle changes. Drinking more tea and water is strongly recommended throughout your 30-day reversion plan, as long as the tea is not peppermint-flavored. Also, in your first week of recovery, be sure to get as much sleep as possible, in conjunction with eating 2 to 3 hours before you sleep. A meal should also be incorporated throughout this entire 30-day stretch. This plan should include egg whites in the morning, instead of coffee switch to tea for your caffeine fix. For lunch, whole grain bread with lean meat- chicken or turkey preferably- with light sauce and a bevy of vegetables. Moreover, dinner should include a balanced meal that provides nutrients and foods that will not induce heartburn. Remember, this meal should be consumed a few hours before bed so that your body has time to properly digest the food. Also, be sure to refrain from lying directly on your back after your meal; as mentioned, this will induce acid reflux symptoms like heartburn and excess bloating.

In week 2, in keeping with the consumption of nutrient-rich food and water consumption from the previous week, you should begin an exercise routine of you have been devoid of routine prior to week 2. A consistent exercise routine will help maintain overall health so that your body has excess strength and energy to overcome the wear and damage inflicted from GERD symptoms. Also, a consistent exercise routine will boost your metabolism so that you can burn off excess unhealthy fats and complex carbohydrates that can cause strain to your body and induce reflux symptoms. In the third week of your 30-day revision plan, you can slightly increase the size of your meals. Still, make sure that the overall size of your meals remain relatively small, with only slight additions where you may see fit. By week three, your exercise routine, water consumption, and sleep habits should be starting to feel more routine and many of reflux your symptoms will begin to diminish. Moreover, leading into week 4, your diet should continue to incorporate nuts, vegetables, fruits, tea, and other plant-based foods and drinks to expedite the healing process. However, the final week of your 30-day recovery plan is vital for sustaining the progress that you have presumably made since the start of the month. It is vital because you must ensure that you do not get too comfortable in your routine that you allow for gradual decline back into the habits that spawned your acid reflux. Pushing through this final week will augment your progress and solidify your path to living a reflux-free life. Specifically, with regard to your diet, you can incorporate the following fruit and vegetable smoothie recipe. Smoothies and healthy shakes are an excellent meal replacement option for optimal health and recovery from acid reflux.

Add 2 scoops of frozen berries into a 400ml cup
Add 2 scoops of spinach from a 250ml scoop
Add 2 tablespoons of Chia Seeds
Add 2 tablespoons of hemp hearts
Add 1 tablespoon of peanut butter

This smoothie should be blended with water to ensure that it is not excessively thick.

PART 3

Chapter 1: Is Weight Loss Surgery Right for You?

Gastric sleeve surgeries are some of the most life-changing medical procedures a person can go through. The results are often dramatic weight loss and a decrease in health risks. Of course, this type of surgery is a better choice for some people than it is for others. How do you know if you could be a potential candidate for weight loss surgery? The rest of this chapter will provide details about whether bariatric weight loss surgery may be a good option for you.

Guidelines

In order to be considered as a candidate for gastric bypass surgeries, you generally need to have already exhausted other methods for losing weight. Your doctor will most likely ask you about your typical diet, as well as diets and exercises that you have tried in the past. He or she will also need information about your current exercise routine. Your general health and risks of obesity-related health issues will be taken into account as well. In most cases, your BMI (body mass index) must be at least 40 in order to be a candidate for surgery. Sometimes, people who have a BMI of at least 35 are considered. Typically, with the lower BMI of 35, you also have obesity-related severe medical issues such as type 2 diabetes or persistent high blood pressure.

In addition to these guidelines, you will go through the screening processes to determine if weight loss surgery is the best option for you as an individual. The medical team wants to be sure that the surgery will be beneficial to you and that the risks are outweighed by the benefits. Other factors that the medical team will look at are your psychiatric profile, your age, and the level of motivation that you show to become a healthier person with the assistance of bariatric surgery. Surgeries can be performed on teenagers if the benefits greatly outweigh the risks. Bariatric surgeries have also been performed on people who are aged 60 years and over if the benefits are greater than the risks associated with surgery and anesthesia. Prior to surgery, you may be required to show proof that you have made changes to your lifestyle in terms of diet and exercise in preparation for life after your gastric sleeve surgery.

Are you ready for surgery?

Aside from the medical perspective on things, you will have many other questions to ask yourself before deciding if you are ready to go through with a life-altering surgical procedure. You will need to determine how to pay for the procedure. If you have health insurance, you must first receive a pre-approval in order to know what will be covered by the insurance company, and what, if any, portion of the expenses you will be required to cover.

You also have to understand that the surgery itself is not a magical solution. It is only one of the many tools you will use to reach your goal of a healthier lifestyle at a lower weight. In order to reach your full potential after surgery, you will need to be dedicated to a healthier lifestyle. You will have to make nutritional changes to your diet, and you have to start exercising regularly or increase exercise if you are already active. There is also a high probability that you will need to take multivitamins and other supplements, as bariatric surgeries inhibit your body's ability to absorb nutrients.

There are some other points to consider when questioning bariatric surgery for weight loss. People who have struggled with alcohol or medicinal addiction in the past may not be good candidates for gastric bypass surgeries. Similarly, cigarette smokers will need to quit smoking many months before surgery. You will be required to enroll in educational classes before your surgery. Some of these classes will be for you to learn about proper nutrition. This means that you must be able to make time to attend the classes. Some of the screenings that you go through prior to scheduling a surgery may include imaging studies that will monitor your digestive system, as well as blood tests.

Risks associated with surgery

All surgeries have risks that are associated with them that may occur during or after surgery. Weight loss surgeries are no different, and your medical team will help you to measure the benefits and the risks. You will most likely have low levels of calcium, iron, vitamins, and minerals after surgery. This issue can be easily prevented or solved by the addition of daily multivitamins and other necessary supplements. You may experience something called dumping syndrome, which has symptoms of nausea, vomiting, diarrhea, and abdominal cramping. Your intestines may narrow in the areas in which surgery was performed. These narrowed areas are called strictures. If you do not follow recommendations, you may not lose weight or may gain weight back after it is lost. You may also develop a need for another related surgery. Speaking with your doctor will help you determine if you may be a good candidate and if the timing is right for you to undergo a surgery.

Key Points

- Weight loss surgeries are life-changing procedures.
- Surgery in and of itself is not a solution. It is merely a tool that you use in attaining weight loss and a healthier lifestyle.
- You will need to change your eating habits and exercise habits to benefit from surgery.
- You must go through the screening processes to determine if you are a good candidate and which type of surgery will be most beneficial to you.
- The screening processes may include blood testing and imaging sessions.
- You should also consider the financial aspects of surgery, as it can be quite expensive and may or may not be covered by health insurance.
- You will be required to attend educational sessions prior to your surgery to learn about proper nutrition, among other learning opportunities.
- There are risks associated with bariatric surgeries, as with all surgeries. Your doctor will help you determine if the benefits are greater than the associated risks.

Chapter 2: Types of Gastric Sleeve Surgeries

There are four types of gastric bypass surgeries that are among the most commonly performed for weight loss purposes. Each of these kinds of surgeries has associated positive and negative components. There are similarities and differences between the various surgery choices. The four types will be explained below.

It is important to remember that all types of gastric bypass surgery will require changes in diet and exercise in order to reduce health risks and to be successful. You may need to begin taking a daily multivitamin or other supplements due to nutrient absorption issues. You will have the best and healthiest results by working closely with your doctor or surgeon to decide which surgery is right for you, and what your postoperative lifestyle should be like.

Sleeve Gastrectomy

Sleeve gastrectomy limits the size of the stomach by removing a part of it laparoscopically. It works by affecting the amount of food that can be consumed. As a result of the surgery, the hormones are also affected and will assist in the process of losing weight. A benefit is that the hormonal changes can also trigger changes in blood pressure, which will help prevent heart disease. Approximately 80 percent of the stomach is cut away during the surgery, and the organ is left in a tubular shape. The new functional stomach is much smaller than before surgery. Since this is the case, much smaller food portions will be eaten, reducing the overall caloric intake. This option is typically available for people who have a BMI (body mass index) of at least 40. Having this surgery can help you to lose weight and reduce your risk of life-threatening health issues caused by obesity. (Mayo Clinic, n.d.)

Duodenal Switch with Biliopancreatic Diversion

This surgery has two parts. The first part is similar to a sleeve gastrectomy, which removes approximately 80 percent of the stomach. The difference in this surgery is that the pyloric valve that releases food from the stomach is not removed, nor is the duodenum. These two parts will remain in the body. The duodenum is the part of the intestines to which the stomach connects. The second part of this surgery connects the end portion of the intestines to the duodenum. This will cause a reduction in the amount of food that you can consume. It also causes a reduction in the number of nutrients that can be absorbed by the body.

As with sleeve gastrectomy, the new stomach is much smaller, this causes smaller portions to be ingested. The use of less of the intestines contributes to weight loss by reducing the overall absorption of nutrients. The majority of nutrients pass through the digestive system before they are effectively absorbed. This type of surgery is less common than sleeve gastrectomy. It is reserved for people with a BMI of at least 50. The surgery can only be an option if you have already unsuccessfully tried diet and exercise changes to attempt weight loss. It will help you to lose weight and lessen your risk of obesity-related health concerns. (Mayo Clinic, n.d.)

Laparoscopic Adjustable Gastric Banding

The stomach's top section is wrapped around in an adjustable band in this type of surgery. Only a small pouch of the former stomach will remain functional, allowing you to eat less and lose weight. There will be a port placed under your abdominal skin that will allow for the band to adjust. Adjustments are made to the fluid content of a balloon that has been placed under the band. Your doctor can make these changes at appointments, by inserting a needle into the port to add or decrease the amount of fluid that the balloon holds. As with the prior two surgeries, this one also is effective because the functioning amount of the stomach is much smaller. The biggest difference is that the amount of stomach that is portioned off can be adjusted after the surgery is complete. This choice is best for people with a BMI between 40 and 50. If your BMI is over 50, you may not lose as much weight as you desire with this option. (John Hopkins Medicine Health Library, n.d.)

Roux-En-Y Gastric Bypass

This is somewhat the same with the gastric banding but does not specifically use a sleeve or band. It is included here for comparison purposes because it is a common type of bariatric surgery and it also ultimately reduces the size of the stomach. The upper portion of the stomach is stapled off. The result is a pouch that is the size of a chicken egg. The new pouch is attached directly to the intestines, creating a "y" shape. This surgery will help you lose weight by reducing the number of calories and fat that you absorb from foods, along with a reduction in the absorption of minerals and vitamins. After having this surgery, you will be on a modified diet. It will be approximately one-month post surgery before you are able to return to eating normal foods. This option is best for people with a BMI of at least 40. (John Hopkins Medicine Health Library, n.d.)

Key Points

- All gastric sleeve surgeries have risks and benefits associated with them.
- There are similarities that are common factors in the surgeries that are offered, but each surgery has its own sets of positive and negative aspects.
- Most gastric bypass surgeries are performed laparoscopically.
- The duodenal switch with biliopancreatic diversion is ideal for people with a BMI of at least 50. The rest of the commonly performed gastric banding surgeries are ideal for those with a BMI of at least 40.
- Roux-en-Y gastric bypass surgery and duodenal switch with biliopancreatic diversion surgery reduce the absorption of nutrients.
- Laparoscopic adjustable gastric banding allows for adjustments to stomach size to be made by your doctor. You will also be left with a port after surgery so that the adjustments can be completed.
- Discussion with your doctor will help you to determine which surgical choice is best for you.

Chapter 3: The Recovery Phase

Following gastric sleeve surgery, your life will likely look much different than before you started your process as a candidate for the procedure. You will have to take especially good care of yourself and attend all post-op appointments. You will also learn to eat nutritiously with a smaller stomach and developing new exercise routines.

Post-Operative Care

You may spend the first one or two days after surgery in the hospital. This is an excellent time to review any question you might have with your doctor. You might want to go over things such as pain medications, returning to your normal activities, and care for your surgical incision.

You should let your doctor know immediately if you experience any symptoms that could be a result of your surgery. These include a fever, difficulty in breathing, abdominal pain, vomiting, diarrhea, or an incision that feels hot or painful. These could also be signs of infection.

For the first couple of weeks following surgery, you will probably only be permitted to consume a liquid diet. Once you begin to eat regular foods, you must remember to eat slowly while chewing your food well. You will also need to refrain from drinking for a half hour before you eat and for one-half hour after eating.

Nutritional absorption issues may develop after a bariatric surgery. Your doctor will help you to prevent this by telling you to take multivitamins and supplements each day. In addition to a general multivitamin, you may be advised to also take calcium and iron supplements, as well as vitamins D and B12. For the rest of your life, you will most likely take blood tests twice yearly to ascertain your nutritional levels and to determine if any changes should be made to the supplements that you take.

Foods That Promote Recovery and Healing

Some foods are healthier choices than others. After undergoing a weight loss procedure, it is very important to opt for nutrient dense foods that will meet the needs of your diet. There are some foods that are especially noted for their restorative and healing properties such as foods that are high in antioxidants and vitamins. Foods that are rich in vitamins A, C, and D are especially beneficial in aiding healing after surgery. Foods with high levels of vitamin A include dark green vegetables like kale and spinach and orange vegetables like sweet potatoes and carrots. Berries, oranges, melons, tomatoes, and bell peppers are all vitamin C rich. Vitamin D can be found in fish, eggs, milk, and some cereals. Grapes, pomegranates, and all types of berries are full of antioxidants. Antioxidant repair damage to the body. Healthy fats such as nuts, avocado, and olive oil can help your body absorb the vitamins it needs to heal properly. Other highly nutritious foods to ensure you are eating include bok choy, seafood, eggs, beans, and whole grains. Bok choy can contribute to your vitamin K intake, seafood and eggs deliver protein, and beans and whole grains will keep your energy levels up. Yogurt will provide healthy probiotics that will help you with digestion.

Getting In and Staying In Shape with Exercise

Getting proper nutrition is only half the battle in gaining a new healthier lifestyle after weight loss surgery. You will also need to determine what types of exercise will benefit you most and develop a workout routine. You will likely combine some sort of cardio and weight training activities. Always discuss with your medical team to ascertain a safe time to begin adding workouts to your schedule.

Swimming, cycling, and walking are generally the best places to start for low-intensity cardio or aerobic exercises. You will slowly increase your daily activity to add in a stroll through the park, or using the stairs instead of an elevator. Once you get started, you will have an eventual goal of 60 minutes of moderate exercise. Low-intensity exercise is best for weight loss. You will want to exercise on most days, but it is important to take approximately one day a week off to allow your body to rest and make any needed repairs. If you ever feel joint pain, that is not a typical result, and you should make alterations to your exercising routine. The majority of exercise that you do should be of the cardio or aerobic variety, but it is good to add in about 15 minutes of weight training or strength training as well.

Weight training or strength training is fine to add to your workouts up to three times each week. However, you will want to make sure that you space the sessions out by a minimum of 48 hours. Start off slow with light weights and build up as you progress. It is better to have more repetitions than heavier weights to reach a weight loss goal. Lastly, make sure that you are switching up your workouts every six weeks or so. Your body can become complacent with the same exercise routine for long periods of time, so changes are needed to keep your weight loss going.

Key Points

- After your surgery, you will most likely have a short hospital stay.
- Consult with your doctor for the answers to any questions that you may have.
- Be on the lookout for any symptoms of infection.
- Difficulty in the absorption of nutrients is a known side effect of bariatric procedures.
- Nutritional supplements and multivitamins can help to offset difficulty in absorbing needed nutrients.
- Eat small, healthy portions of nutrient dense foods.
- Foods that are rich in protein, antioxidants, and vitamins will be the best for helping you heal after surgery.
- Probiotics are beneficial for digestion.
- Exercise when you have the go-ahead from your doctor.
- Add physical activity slowly.
- Start with light cardio activities and increase exercise until you have six days a week of 60-minute aerobic intervals.
- Adding in weight training or strength training can aid in losing weight and building lean muscle.
- Switch up workout routines often to continue losing weight.

Chapter 4: Recipes for Recovery

While recovering from gastric bypass surgery, you need to be assured that you are receiving adequate nutrients such as vitamins and protein. You will also be eating smaller portions than you are used to after obtaining a gastric sleeve. In order to recover healthfully, it is necessary to eat nutritious foods in variety.

The recipes contained within this book have all been developed especially for patients who have undergone gastric sleeve surgeries. In addition, these recipes contain ingredients that are known to promote healing and recovery and contain nutrition information at the end of each. The serving sizes are all small portions and the foods are delicious. You will find options for breakfasts, lunches, dinners, snacks, and even desserts. Start exploring and choose your favorites!

Egg Muffins

This delicious recipe can be prepped ahead for breakfast on-the-go. Eggs and turkey bacon provide protein to promote healing.

Ingredients:

- Black pepper, .25 teaspoons
- Salt, .25 teaspoons
- 1% milk, .5 c
- Shredded cheese, low fat, .75 c
- Turkey bacon, precooked, 12 slices
- Eggs, 6 large

Preparation Method:

1. Set your oven to 350 degrees.
2. Put one crumbled bacon slice at the bottom of one of the muffin cups of a muffin tin.
3. Except for the cheese, mix all of the other ingredients together.
4. Put .25 c of the mixture in each muffin cup.
5. Sprinkle the shredded cheese over the tops of the muffins.
6. Bake the egg muffins for 20 to 25 minutes.

Number of servings: 12

Size of serving: 1 muffin

- 98 calories
- 7 grams fat
- 2 grams saturated fat
- 1 gram carbohydrates
- 0 gram fiber
- 1 gram sugar
- 8 grams protein

Breakfast Berry Wrap

Berries provide antioxidants needed for healing and whole grains for energy. This breakfast can be prepared quickly and easily, no baking required.

Ingredients:

- Sliced strawberries, fresh, .25 c
- Strawberry jelly, low sugar, 1 Tablespoon
- Ricotta cheese, 3 Tablespoons
- Whole wheat tortilla, 1

Preparation Method:

1. Spread the jelly and the ricotta cheese on the tortilla.
2. Sprinkle the strawberries.
3. Roll the tortilla up and serve.

Serving size: 1 wrap

Number of servings: 1

- 229 milligrams sodium
- 233 calories
- 24 milligrams cholesterol
- 30 grams carbohydrates
- 9 grams fat
- 8 grams sugar
- 8 grams protein

Black Bean and Corn Salad

A delightful mixture of beans and corn will provide protein and energy. There is no cooking necessary, so this recipe is easy enough for anyone to try out.

Ingredients:

- Whole kernel corn, 1 cup
- Lemon juice, 1 teaspoon
- Minced garlic, 1 teaspoon
- Olive oil, 2 Tablespoons
- Honey, 1 teaspoon
- Black pepper, .25 teaspoons
- Minced red onion, 2 Tablespoons
- Balsamic vinegar, .25 cups
- Drained and rinsed black beans, (2) 16 oz cans
- Fresh parsley, .25 cups

Preparation Method:

1. Mix the corn, black beans, red onion, and pepper in a large mixing dish.
2. All of the other ingredients should be whisked.
3. Pour the liquids over the mixture.
4. Marinate the salad for 30 minutes before serving.

Serving size: .25 c

Number of servings: 6

- 306 milligrams potassium
- 40 milligrams sodium
- 0 milligram cholesterol
- 6 grams protein
- 3 grams sugar
- 6 grams fiber
- 23 grams g carbohydrates
- 5 grams fat
- 160 calories

Baked Chicken and Vegetables

A classic dinner takes on a new life in this recipe. Cook dinner for the family or meal prep and have this recipe for lunches and dinners. Protein and vitamin A will aid in the recovery.

Ingredients:

- Black pepper, .25 t
- Thyme, 1 teaspoon
- Water, .5 c
- Raw skinless chicken, 1
- Quartered onion, 1 large
- Sliced carrots, 6
- Sliced potatoes, 4

Preparation Method:

1. Preheat your oven to 400 degrees.
2. Put the carrots, potatoes, and onions in a large oven-safe dish.
3. Place the chicken over the vegetables.
4. Mix up the water, black pepper, and thyme.
5. Pour this mixture over the vegetables and chicken.
6. Spoon the cooking juices over the chicken two times while cooking. Bake for at least one hour until the chicken is browned.

Serving size: one-sixth of the recipe

Number of servings: 6

- 130 milligram sodium

- 26 grams protein
- 10 grams sugar
- 4grams fiber
- 25 gram carbohydrates
- 3.5 gram fat
- 240 calories

Asian Style Lettuce Wraps

Full of flavor, this recipe provides you with plenty of protein! This one is great for a group or as a make-ahead meal.

Ingredients:

- Sliced cucumber, 1 small
- Chopped green onion, 1 whole
- Butter lettuce, 8 leaves
- Sesame oil, toasted, 1 teaspoon
- Minced ginger, 1 teaspoon
- Ground chicken breast, .5 lb
- Minced onion, 1 c
- Minced garlic, 1 Tablespoon
- Splenda, 2 packets
- Sriracha hot sauce, 2 teaspoon
- Peanut butter, unsalted, 1 Tablespoon
- Soy sauce, low sodium, 2 teaspoons
- Hoisin sauce, 2 Tablespoons

Preparation Method:

1. Combine hoisin sauce, sriracha, peanut butter, soy sauce, and Splenda in a bowl and mix well.
2. Place a nonstick skillet over medium heat.
3. Cook the onion for four minutes. Mix in the garlic and cook for one more minute.
4. Add the ground chicken and ginger.
5. Increase the temperature of the burner to medium-high heat.
6. Break the chicken up and cook it until there is no pink color left.
7. Stir the sesame oil in and remove from the heat.
8. Divide the product evenly among the lettuce leaves.
9. Top with cucumber and green onion.

Serving size: 2 wraps

Number of servings: 4

- 637 milligrams sodium
- 33 milligrams cholesterol
- 16 grams protein
- 4 grams sugar
- 5 grams fiber
- 11 grams carbohydrates
- 4 grams fat
- 155 calories

Cheesesteak Wrap

Yes, you can still enjoy a chicken cheesesteak. With a few tweaks to the original, this recipe contains protein, vitamin C, and antioxidants.

Ingredients:

- Low carb tortilla, 1
- Light Swiss cheese, .75 oz
- Sliced mushrooms, .25 c
- Sliced green peppers, .25 c
- Chopped onions, .25 c
- Skinless, boneless chicken breast, .25 lb

Preparation Method:

1. Pound the chicken breast until it is .25 inch thin. Then create thin strips by cutting it with a knife.
2. Cook the chicken on the medium-high heat in a cooking pan with the onions.
3. Add the mushrooms and the green pepper and continue cooking.
4. Warm the tortilla for 20 seconds in the microwave, then place in the middle of two damp paper towels.
5. Spread the cheese in the middle of the tortilla.
6. Add the vegetables and the chicken.
7. Fold up the tortilla and serve.

Serving size: 1 wrap

Number of servings: 1

- 620 milligrams sodium
- 76 milligrams cholesterol
- 3 grams protein
- 4 grams fiber
- 264 calories
- 17 grams carbohydrates
- 6 grams fat

Beef Ginger Stir Fry

Instead of going out, try to make a stir-fry for you at home. This recipe provides plenty of protein, vitamin A, and whole grains for energy.

Ingredients:

- Water chestnuts, 8 oz
- Bok choy, 2 medium stalks, cut in .5 inch slices
- Brown rice, instant, .5 c
- Medium bell pepper, .5 cut in strips
- Broccoli florets, 3 oz
- Red pepper flakes, crushed, .25 teaspoons
- Soy sauce, 3 Tablespoons
- Cornstarch, 1 Tablespoon
- Canola oil, 1 teaspoon
- Beef broth, 6 oz fat-free
- Garlic cloves, 2 medium
- Ground ginger, 2 teaspoon
- Flank steak, 1 lb (in .25 inch strips)

Preparation Method:

1. Mix the garlic, ginger, and steak slices in a bowl and set it aside.
2. Stir the broth, soy sauce, and cornstarch together in a separate bowl.
3. Heat the oil in a skillet over medium-high heat. Add the pepper flakes.

4. Constantly stir the steak while cooking it for four to five minutes, and then set it aside.
5. Cook the bell pepper and broccoli for two to three minutes. Then add the water chestnuts and the bok choy.
6. In the center of the pan, make a well to put in the broth.
7. Cook this for one to two minutes, and then mix the beef in and cook for an additional one to two minutes.
8. Serve the stir-fry over the rice.

Serving size: .25 of the total

Number of servings: 4

- 17 grams protein
- 6 grams sugar
- 2 grams fiber
- 25 grams carbohydrates
- 8 grams fat
- 275 calories

Zucchini Boats

Chock full of antioxidants and protein, this recipe will assist in healing. It makes many servings, so this is a good recipe for making ahead or for a family dinner.

Ingredients:

- Low-fat shredded mozzarella cheese, 1 c
- Black pepper, .25 t
- Whole wheat bread crumbs, .25 c
- Spaghetti sauce, .75 c
- Diced tomato, 1 large
- Sliced mushrooms, .5 lb
- Beaten egg, 1
- Chopped onion, .5 c
- Ground turkey, 1 lb
- Zucchini, 4 medium

Preparation Method:

1. Slice the zucchinis lengthwise in half. Scoop out the pulp to create boats and set it aside.
2. Put the boats in a large dish safe for use in the microwave. Cover the dish, and then heat it in the microwave for three minutes on high.
3. In a skillet, cook the onion and turkey on the medium-high heat.
4. Drain the turkey mix.

5. Mix the zucchini pulp, egg, bread crumbs, spaghetti sauce, tomato, mushrooms, cheese, pepper, and turkey mix.
6. Place a quarter cup of the mix into each one of the shells.
7. Bake for 20 minutes, uncovered, at 350 degrees.

Serving size: 1 boat

Number of servings: 8

- 294 milligrams sodium
- 17.5 grams protein
- 5 grams sugar
- 4 grams fiber
- 16 grams carbohydrates
- 7.5 grams fat
- 195 calories

Veggie Pizza

This recipe is fun for parties or an evening at home. Plenty of vegetables make it great for recovery and healing.

Ingredients:

- Black olives, .5 c sliced
- Shredded Colby jack cheese, low fat .75c
- Diced cucumbers, .25 c
- Diced green pepper, .25 c
- Diced tomatoes, .25 c
- Diced broccoli, raw .75 c
- Shredded carrots, .25 c
- Ranch dressing dry mix, 1 package
- Sour cream, low fat, .5 c
- Cream cheese, low fat, .5c
- Large low carb wraps 2

Preparation Method:

1. Mix the ranch dry mix, sour cream, and cream cheese until combined.
2. Spread the ranch combination on the tortillas.
3. Use the vegetables as toppings.
4. Sprinkle the cheese over the top.
5. Divide the tortillas into quarters and serve.

Serving size: .25 tortilla

Number of servings: 8

- 870 milligrams sodium
- 23 milligrams cholesterol
- 10 grams protein
- 1.6 grams sugar
- 4 grams fiber
- 12 grams carbohydrates
- 10 grams fat
- 170 calories

Hummus

This is a classic hummus recipe. Use it for a vegetable dip or for salads.

Ingredients:

- Salt, .5 teaspoon
- Chickpeas, (1) 15 oz can rinsed
- Lemon juice, 3 Tablespoons
- Olive oil, 3 Tablespoons
- Tahini, 1 Tablespoon
- Garlic, clove 1 peeled

Preparation Method:

1. Chop the garlic in a food processor.
2. Add all of the other listed ingredients.
3. Blend the ingredients one to two minutes, until entirely smooth.

Serving size: 2

Number of servings: 12

- 149 milligrams sodium
- 0 milligram cholesterol
- 6 grams protein
- 0 gram sugar
- 72 calories
- 7.5 grams carbohydrates
- 4.5 grams fat

Spicy Devilled Eggs

This is a great snack to have on hand for a little protein. You can make it ahead and have it ready.

Ingredients:

- Paprika a dash
- Black pepper a dash
- Hard boiled eggs, 6 whites, 3 yolks
- Dijon mustard .25 t
- Dill .5 t
- Greek yogurt 2 T

Preparation Method:

1. Peel all of the eggs and slice them lengthwise in half.
2. Set aside the whites. Put three yolks in a bowl to mix.
3. Mash the yolks with the yogurt, dijon, and dill.
4. Spoon the filling in the half eggs.
5. Sprinkle paprika and black pepper on the tops of the eggs.

Serving size: 2 egg halves

Number of servings: 3

- 219 milligrams sodium
- 225 milligrams cholesterol
- 10 grams protein
- 0 gram sugar
- 131 calories
- 1 gram carbohydrates
- 8.7 grams fat

Soy Chocolate Dessert

This is a recipe for a pudding made with tofu. The tofu makes the dessert creamy and healthy, and the protein helps you heal.

Ingredients:

- Vanilla extract, .5 t
- Silken tofu, 16 oz
- Skim milk, 1 c
- Fat-free, sugar-free chocolate fudge pudding, instant, 1 package
- Hot water, .25 c
- Unflavored gelatin, 1 envelope

Preparation Method:

1. Mix the hot water and gelatin in a small bowl and allow it to set.
2. Dice the tofu in one-inch cubes and put it in a mixing bowl with the pudding.
3. Add vanilla extract and place the mixture in a blender.
4. Blend until you reach a smooth texture, and then add the gelatin gradually until well-combined. Blend once more.
5. Pour the mix in an 8-inch by 8-inch dish.
6. Cover and leave the dish in the refrigerator for at least 30 minutes.

Serving size: .5 c

Number of servings: 8

- 181 milligrams sodium

- 1 milligram cholesterol
- 5 grams protein
- 6 grams carbohydrates
- 1 grams fat
- 56 calories

Cheesecake Pudding

Here is a dessert that takes no time at all to make. Greek yogurt provides protein that is needed for the healing process.

Ingredients:

- Cheesecake flavored pudding mix 1 packet, sugar-free
- Greek yogurt 1 c, plain, fat-free

Preparation Method:

1. In a blender, puree the ingredients until they are combined.

Serving size: .5 c

Number of servings: 2

- 7 grams protein
- 4.5 grams sugar
- 3 grams carbohydrates
- 0 grams fat
- 62 calories

Conclusion

The next step is to choose some of the recipes that appeal to you and start cooking! If you have completed your bariatric surgery, please be sure that you follow all post-operative instructions from your doctor or surgeon. If you have yet to complete your surgery, then take this time to try out a few of the recipes in this book and choose your favorites. You can go grocery shopping and be stocked up on all of the ingredients you will need after your surgery. You might even decide to cook ahead of time and make some freezer meals that will be easy to reheat after your surgery is complete. After your weight loss surgery, you will be making a complete lifestyle change. To that end, all of the recipes are suitable for meal prepping and can benefit you in packing breakfasts, lunches, and snacks that you can take along with you if you go to work or school.

Addressing the symptoms, in this manner, will allow your body to fight off disease like GERD and Barrett's disease as soon as possible rather than at a later time when your body is significantly weaker. Keep in mind that the best method of addressing your symptoms is to consult a medical professional. In this way, you can begin to implement the strategies presented in this book with guidance from a qualified medical professional.

Given that your acid reflux is likely to exist on a ranging spectrum and will most definitely be different for every individual, this book provides methods of addressing your symptoms and ailments in a manner that is applicable and helpful for whichever stage of the reflux you are experiencing. What's more, the 30-day recovery plan is a great way to ensure that your symptoms are staved off for good once you can utilize medical intervention. If, for instance, you are prescribed drugs to mitigate your symptoms, be sure to use the methods outlined in this book in conjunction with the prescribed amount of medication that your doctor has instructed.

Where your health is concerned, being prepared and informed is critical to seeing that you successfully overcome the ailments that are affecting you.

That is precisely why this book is of value. After reading, you are now informed about the intricate aspects of acid reflux and should feel extremely prepared as you move forward in addressing these symptoms.

www.ingramcontent.com/pod-product-compliance
Lightning Source LLC
Chambersburg PA
CBHW071518080526
44588CB00011B/1469